The God Between Us

○

"Creating stories within stories is tricky with scripture. We know the plots and characters so well, and our attachments to them can be fierce. If someone is going to mess with them, they'd better do it eloquently and affectionately. Lyn Brakeman does both. These six wonderful midrashes crack open their founding stories in wonderful, faithful ways, and God is known precisely between the ancient narrative and these lovely modern parables."

> Dr. John Fortunato, Clinical Psychologist;
> Author of *Embracing the Exile* and *AIDS: The Spiritual Dilemma*

"Rev. Lyn Brakeman 'reads between the lines' of Sacred Scripture and discovers there the beauty and depth of God-in-Us. The 'old' stories are renewed with fresh insight and imagination. She story-tells with wonder and grace, lament and laughter!"

> Rev. Robert VerEeke, S.J., Pastor, St. Ignatius Church, Chestnut Hill, MA;
> Author of *Ritual Plays: Engaging Communities in God's Work*

○

Also available by Lyn Brakeman:

Spiritual Lemons:
Biblical Women, Irreverent Laughter, and Righteous Rage
(Innisfree Press, 1997)

The God Between Us

A Spirituality of Relationships

Lyn Brakeman

Innisfree
Press, Inc.

*A call to the
deep heart's core*

Published by Innisfree Press, Inc.
136 Roumfort Road
Philadelphia, PA 19119
800-367-5872
Visit our website at www.InnisfreePress.com.

Cover design by Hugh Duffy, PhD Design, Carneys Point, NJ

Library of Congress Cataloging-in-Publication Data
Brakeman, Lyn.
   The God between us : a spirituality of relationships /
Lyn Brakeman.
      p. cm.
   ISBN 1-880913-54-2
      1. Women in the Bible—Meditations. 2. Interpersonal
   relations—Religious aspects—Meditations. I. Title.
BS575.B635 2001
242'.5—dc21   2001039743

Portions of this book appeared earlier in *The Other Side* magazine as "God In Between," Nov/Dec 2000.

All scripture quotations are taken from the *New Revised Standard Version Bible.* Copyright © 1989 by the Division of Christian Education of the National Council of the Churches of Christ in the U.S.A. Used by permission. All rights reserved.

Quotation from *Anam Cara: A Book of Celtic Wisdom* by John O'Donohue, copyright © 1997 by John O'Donohue, are reprinted by permission of HarperCollins Publishers, Inc.

Quotation from "My Mother's Body," *The Art of Blessing the Day: Poems with a Jewish Theme* by Marge Piercy, copyright © 1999 by Middlemarsh, Inc., are reprinted by permission of Alfred A. Knopf.

Quotation from *Genesis: The Beginning of Desire* by Avivah Gottlieb Zornberg, published 1995, are reprinted by permission of The Jewish Publication Society.

Quotation from *The Poisonwood Bible* by Barbara Kingsolver, copyright © 1998 by Barbara Kingsolver, are reprinted by permission of HarperCollins Publishers, Inc.

To Dick, a man generous of spirit
and my marriage partner, best friend, lover, and colleague.

Contents

Introduction . . . 11

The Vow . . . 19
HERODIAS AND SALOME (Mark 6:17-29)
*How can a mother and a daughter forgive the hurt
they have caused one another?*

The Final Petition . . . 48
QUEEN ESTHER AND A PALACE EUNUCH (The Book of Esther)
How can a deeply connected friendship be life-saving?

A Mother's Cry . . . 73
MARY AND JESUS (Mark 15:33-16:15)
*How does a mother resolve her feelings of abandonment
and let go of her child?*

A Different Kind of Love . . . 86
DAVID AND JONATHAN (I Samuel 13:16 - II Samuel 1:1)
How is the love between two men a blessing?

The Garden Restored . . . 110
ADAM AND EVE (Genesis 2:4b-3)
How can a marriage survive a very deep wound?

Idle Tale . . . 137
THE WOMEN AT JESUS' TOMB (Luke 24)
*How is it that when women get together and support each other,
their collective wisdom can make such a difference?*

Acknowledgments

With gratitude, I acknowledge first the prayers, support, and spiritual chutzpah of many friends and colleagues who, with good hearts and good humor, join with me to push the edges of the envelope and color outside the lines.

My publisher and chief editor, Marcia Broucek, has inspired me with her own faith and good spirit through the hard job of making a small press successful in the face of conglomerate giants.

Some people are born with a silver spoon in their mouths, but my on-site editor, Susanna Brougham, was born with a red pencil in hers. Her meticulous attention to editing detail was surpassed only by the gentle grace with which she could suggest that perhaps my most coveted poetics did not really further the action of the story.

I am grateful for the work of Robert McKee whose story-writing course opened my eyes to the need for solid structure in literature. I liken this to making sure there is a well-constructed trellis to support the growth of beautiful roses.

Finally, I thank my iMac for not quitting, even when I forgot to back things up, and to my husband, Dick, for sharing with me—really temporarily deeding to me—the computer. For this and more, I dedicate this book to him with deep gratitude from me and the God between us.

Introduction

"The Bible is familiar, life is strange.
We bring the two together, to shed light on life."

—Avivah Gottlieb Zornberg,
GENESIS: THE BEGINNING OF DESIRE

The Bible drives me nuts. It also keeps me sane. It's hard to live with. And even harder to live without. It's inconsistent, incomprehensible, inhospitable to women, and, for the most part, much too busy for contemplative prayer. But I'm in love with it, and I blame God for the whole love affair, God who taught me that the central character of the Bible is neither God nor humanity, but their relationship.

This God lives and works in the spaces between us, spaces we imagine are empty but are really crackling with connective energy. I do not proclaim a new deity; I am a monotheist. But because of my biblical love affair, I have learned and experienced the dynamics of the one God in new ways.

I think of this "God Between" in feminine images. She is an active spirit, able to do many things at once: kiss a baby's brow, smear jelly on a schoolchild's sandwich, snatch a sniff of rich coffee, and pull a comb through her hair as she glides past a mirror's edge. She moves with speed but is not in a hurry. She is busy but not burdened. She creates a whole work of art in which everything has its own place and is simultaneously connected with everything else.

She is the Great Connector who has carried my prayers beyond the boundaries of my own self and soul, teaching me that divine spiritual activity is not confined to the individual. She is the star of the biblical narrative who transports love across time and space, pulling for union and reunion. Relationships are her daily bread. She is like a baker woman whose flexed fingers have kneaded and yeasted my relationship with the Bible as well as all my other important relationships. She is the reason I have written this book.

I first met this God Between when I went off to kindergarten. The preparations for the event had been celebrative and encouraging. I even had a new dress and shiny red shoes. But behind my brave smile, I was scared. My mother sent me off with a kiss, a hug, and a word of love, and I felt almost confident as I stepped into the great big world.

Later that day, my fear returned. Someone had looked at me the wrong way, or a teacher had frowned. Suddenly, I felt all alone in a room full of clamoring five-year-olds. Then I remembered, in more than a thought memory, my mother's parting love. I remembered it in my body: her kiss on my cheek and her words in my ear, replacing the cold clutch of my anxiety. The baker-woman God worked in me, leavening the love between me and my mother, keeping it fresh, and transporting it at just the right time into my flesh. There it rose like dough and reconnected me with love and the faith to go on.

My next significant encounter with this God Between came in seventh grade. I was drawn to the Bible and actually read it cover to cover. (Well, maybe I left out parts of Leviticus.) This was a serious endeavor for an early teen; if one of my children had done that, I might have worried! I thought I'd find "something" there and felt crushed to find "nothing."

I realized, in time, that I had come at my task with a compulsive spirit. I read alone, selfishly searching for proofs of my own goodness, solutions to my own problems. I uttered no conscious prayer, asked for no guidance, and didn't think much about God. God, however, working in the in-between to forge an irresistible love connection through the scriptural stories, must have thought about me. In spite of my youthful compulsions, I learned about relationships between faithful people and God. God's people, like me, did strange things. They built arks and dropped everything to follow a guy from Galilee. Also like me, they made tons of mistakes but still belonged. They kept trying to get it right and never gave up on God or themselves—again, like me.

The God I began discovering in the Bible didn't square with the definitions I had memorized in Sunday school. I had received little award pins for my memory work, but those definitions of God—Spirit, infinite, eternal, omnipotent, and other *omni* words—left me with a God who was omni-unreachable and omni-untouchable. This was not the God who had delivered my mother's love into my scared heart at age five. This was not even the biblical God I'd met in seventh grade, the one whose intimate involvement with my ancient brothers and sisters was far from inaccessible.

To my delight, I was finding out that the God of the Bible was moody, like a teenager, always in the middle of things, scrapping with people, and then wooing them back with fierce passion. Best of all, the Bible's God never gave up on the covenant relationship with the people, nor they on God. They always got back together.

How did it work? Could it work for me? Charmed and perplexed by this biblical pattern of connection/disconnection/renewed connection, I wondered if I could trust it in real life.

Wanting to test these ideas, I began to pray intentionally into my relationships, resisting the temptation to pray for myself or the other person, or to ask for change. Instead, I focused on the relationship itself. I knew from my psychological studies that good relationships serve our emotional and spiritual well-being, and that a relationship has a life of its own, larger than individual participants. I also knew from the insights of quantum physics and chaos theory that all things are connected and interdependent, and that connection is not life-stifling but enlivening. Biblically, I knew that the Spirit penetrated and searched everything, even the depths of God (I Corinthians 1:10b). With this knowledge, I prayed, entrusting my relationships to that Spirit and having faith She was at work.

When I prayed about each relationship, I tried to notice what ingredients each person brought to the relationship, what was in the relationship space between us. The space seemed like a rich and nourishing stew whose ingredients included the thoughts, feelings, needs, opinions, wants, and passions of each participant. When ingredients were left out, the stew became thin, lacking in nutrients to feed its participants.

I invited the God Between into some of my stews and prayed for the healing of the relationship itself. For example, if a relationship became taut with fears, I prayed for a massage to oil and soften it. If a relationship was filled with anger and battered, I'd pray that the God Between would be a Good Samaritan to the relationship itself. I found that putting my faith in the God of relationships reduced my anxiety and need for control. Some relationships improved, some had to be let go, but all experienced spiritual transformation. What worked for my faith family in the Bible was working for me.

Avivah Zornberg in her book *Genesis: The Beginning of De-*

sire (The Jewish Publication Society, 1995) speaks of a "hum" in the ears of readers of Scripture, a *hum* that creates an intimate encounter between the reader and the text. I like to think of the God Between as having a tuning fork to the human soul that makes the Bible a living faith journal. All its entries, in history-like fashion, are loosely strung together to reveal a pattern of relationship that kept the biblical people and God connected.

As I read the biblical stories with ears attuned to the *hum*, I found the relationship pattern of connection/disconnection/renewed connection everywhere—in poems and psalms, history and prophecy, teaching and theological discourse. The best part was that the renewed connection was never the same as the original. Each relationship was constantly healing and growing.

One of the ways to listen for the *hum* is through the literary genre of midrash. Midrash, according to Zornberg, honors the thematic integrity of a biblical narrative while drawing new meanings and insights from its text—ideas that stir the human heart today. Literary midrash, unlike scholarly, rabbinical midrash, does not research the interpretive history of a text; however, its imaginative, searching spirit is the same. Doing midrash is taking a text, holding it up to the light of your own spiritual consciousness, then turning it and turning it until as much spiritual truth as possible is revealed and reflected between you and the text. In the tradition of Jewish midrash, the powerful rush of the divine spirit flows through every word, thereby freeing it from any possibility of fixity according to a single human interpretation.

In *The God Between Us*, I have written six midrashim, based on six biblical stories—about a mother and daughter, a marriage, a friendship, a mother and son, two men, and a group of women. As I write, I occasionally refer to the divine voice as God-in-David (or whatever the character's name is), rather than "God said . . ." This way of referring to divine speech is used in Zornberg's book and is also an idea from the Celtic spiritual tradition. There is a voice deep within that, when it speaks, no one has ever heard it before, not even the self. This voice feels almost foreign because it does not conform to our usual patterns of thought. Nor does it comply with the unholy din of inner voices that often fill our heads and assault us with "shoulds," "don'ts," "musts," "wont's", "oughts," and "can'ts." The God-in-you voice feels as if it comes from out of left field precisely because, although it is from within you, it also partakes of the transcendent.

At the end of each chapter, I have included a brief commentary to help make contemporary issues explicit. There are suggestions for prayer and reflection for personal use, for conversation with a spiritual mentor, or for small group discussion. I especially encourage you to pray with the stories to help you hear the *hum* of a particular text, inviting the God Between to connect you to its meaning for you. I offer the following guidelines to help you pray with the Spirit, to discern what God's truth might be for you in each story.

Guidelines for Prayer

1) QUIET, PLEASE.

Libraries are quiet. It takes concentration to study and read with care, to meditate, and to listen for deeper spiritual meaning.

2) BREATHE.

When you listen for the *hum* between you and the text, it is important to get relaxed and comfortable. Use your breathing to listen for the breath of the divine spirit.

3) ASK AND FOLLOW.

Let yourself and God in on what's on your mind. You will get a clue by noticing feelings and reactions, negative or positive, that come up for you while reading a story. Such inner movement is often a signal from the God Between. Follow it.

4) JOURNAL.

You may hear God-in-you say a word, offer an insight, or inspire a surprising feeling or thought. You may not know its meaning, but record it briefly in a journal until more is revealed. Nothing may come to you during a focused prayer time, but something may occur to you days later. Stay tuned in.

5) AMEN.

When you have spent time reflecting on a story and its possible meaning for you, end with a familiar prayer or blessing, and then say amen and mean it. This is a way to let your prayer go into the spaces in between where God will continue to knead and yeast your prayer while you go on with your life.

6) SUGGESTIONS FOR PRAYER POSITIONS.

Try out some different ways to pray with your body. By physically adopting a posture of prayer, you can be expressive of your present spiritual state and/or become more aware of it.

- STAND: Adopt a posture that embodies your worthiness before God.

- KNEEL: Adopt a posture that embodies, with humility, your reverence for God's greater glory.

- PRONE: Adopt a posture that embodies vulnerability, perhaps lying on your back with your arms spread.

- PROSTRATE: Adopt a posture that embodies your brokenness and your need to be raised up.

- DANCE, MOVE: Move in a way that embodies the Spirit's mobility and joy.

- SIT: Adopt a posture that embodies peace, restfulness, attentiveness.

- FETAL: Adopt a posture that represents yourself as an infant, nurtured within the divine womb, or curled up safely inside the scroll of the divine word.

- OPEN-HANDED: Adopt a posture that embodies receptivity.

THE VOW

HERODIAS AND SALOME

(Mark 6:17-29)

O

How can a mother and a daughter forgive the hurt
they have caused one another?

O

When Herodias shoved her daughter, Salome, into the banquet area where King Herod and his men were gathered, fate rushed in. It twirled and dipped right along with the array of silk sashes adorning Salome's slight form and swept her into her dance. Her steps, unplanned, one following the next just as her mother had taught her, flowed like magic. She was lost in the graceful twists of her movement.

But as Salome became aware of the sting from the pounding and rubbing of her bare feet on the ground, the tinkling of her jewels, and the leers on the men's faces, terror shot through her. When the music stopped, she looked at the faces of the men watching her, their heads cocked and their mouths skewed in drunken expressions.

'Oh God, what am I doing here?' she thought. 'Herod is calling me to him now. Where is my mother? She would tell me what to do.'

"I am pleased with your fine dance, girl," Herod said. "You know the custom: If I find pleasure in your offering, you may ask for any favor you wish and I will grant it. On this my birthday feast, it is my turn to grant favors. What do you wish, my girl?"

Salome could not move. She stood mute in front of the king, praying for wisdom, anything to get her away from the watchful eyes of Herod and his courtiers. She had been so entranced with all the preparations, the jewelry and ribbons, the paint on her toenails, the scent of sweet nard, she had forgotten to ask her mother the exact favor they needed. Her mother had been going on and on about a "life-and-death mission" they would accomplish together. This dance was supposed to achieve that goal. But whose life were they planning to save? What did death have to do with it?

As Salome paused, Herod's chief advisor leaned over and spoke into the king's ear. "Herod, let the tongue-tied child go. Don't grant favors to such a young one."

Herod considered and then spoke to Salome. "Go and consult your mother. She will advise you in choosing a favor. Then return to me immediately."

Salome turned and ran. Breathless, she rushed into her mother's chamber where she found Herodias on her knees on the floor, eyes closed, fists tight against her chest, her face contorted.

"Mama, Mama! What's wrong? What are you doing?"

"Oh, nothing. I was fearful. You were gone a long time." Herodias jumped up and embraced her daughter, holding her to her breast until Salome pushed her away.

"Mama, we don't have time for this. Herod wants to grant me a favor. I need to know what to ask for!" Then Salome's face softened and her eyes lit up. "Mama, you should have seen me dance. I was dazzling." Salome spun round on one foot and bowed before her mother.

Herodias stood still, smiling, watching her daughter. Then, reaching for Salome's hand, she pulled her close once more and whispered these words into her ear: "Ask for the head of John the Baptist."

"My God, Mama. Mama! Is this your life-and-death mission? We are to commit *murder*? I thought we needed promises of shelter, money, security, things like that. I thought if we just had the king's favor, we could ask for a guarantee that we would not be . . . What, Mother? What did you mean?"

"You are short-sighted, gullible, and young, Salome. A guarantee by Herod's word is not enough. Never trust the promises or the affections of those who have power over you. You don't know what it can be like for women alone. I made a vow to protect you . . . and I will. Realize, Salome, that John the Baptist doesn't think of us when he tells Herod it is unlawful to be married to his brother's wife.[1] Don't you know we could lose all we have if this preacher gets any more influence? This Baptizer is a threat to us, daughter. Herod has imprisoned him, but

[1] The Herod's intermarried without shame. Herod Antipas, the Herod who participated in Jesus' trial and execution, was Herodias' half-uncle. Herodias had been married to Herod Philip. After the couple were exiled and disinherited because of his mother's plot to kill Herod the Great, Herodias persuaded Herod Antipas, half-brother of Philip and inheritor of the throne in Judaea, to divorce his wife and marry her. Herodias' machinations were successful. She deserted Philip, left Rome and, with her daughter Salome, took her place beside Antipas. The plot forced Antipas to take his kingdom to war, defending his territory under attack by the king of Petra, father of Antipas' former wife whom he left for Herodias. In addition, the Jewish community was astir over the incestuous nature of relationships, and John the Baptist was preaching against Antipas for marrying his brother's wife. The scene at the banquet and the beheading of John the Baptist is portrayed in Mark's gospel and is the only biblical mention of Herodias and her daughter.

that's not enough. We have to be sure. Go before the king again and ask for the Baptizer's head. Go!"

Salome felt flooded with emotions but stood her ground. "You're afraid. I can see it in your eyes. You are supposed to be strong and you're not, not at all. I agreed to use my dancing to secure permanent protection for us. I did not agree to murder. Stop pushing me to do this horrible thing, Mama!"

Herodias grasped Salome's shoulders. "We must take this chance. Ask Herod to sever the head. He will do it, the fool, if nothing else but to save face. We women must keep one step ahead of the selfish conniving of men in power. Besides, this mission isn't for me. Think what would happen to you if you were cast out of Herod's court. Why do you think I schemed and fought to secure my position and power as Herod's wife? It was for you, us. Is that wrong? It's John the Baptist's life or ours. Can't you see?"

"Let his blood stain you, not me," Salome shouted and turned away from Herodias who grabbed her, gave her a quick kiss, resisted the temptation to wipe tears from her daughter's eyes, then pushed Salome back toward the inner chamber where Herod waited.

Herodias collapsed onto her bed. "Oh God," she cried into her pillows. "Salome will do my bidding, but . . . " Herodias's mother's words came to her: "*Scheme your schemes, make your plans, wish all your heart's desires and more, but place your hope in the God of your being who is good.*" Though Herodias knew little about the God of her mother's faith, she poured out her thoughts in anguish to this God. "Salome is right. I am afraid, driven by fear. But we could be cast out with no protection and no resources . . . no men. This is for *her*. All I want is to be sure."

Herodias sat straight up, clasping her hand to her mouth. 'What if my daughter hates me for this? That's worse than losing my life.' She groaned and fell back onto the bed, weeping. 'All alone I have steered my destiny well. Father said the world was cruel and hard, and he encouraged me to be wily and strong. Mother said to trust in God and pray. I've tried to do it all.' Tears soaked the memory of her father and her longing for his approval. 'Oh God, make this work!'

○

Salome flung aside the curtain to her mother's room and heaved the bloody head of John the Baptist toward her mother. The platter that bore the head shattered, cracking the air like lightning splitting a tree. The head thudded to the floor, and Salome gave it a vigorous kick, making sure it would come to rest at her mother's feet.

Herodias shrieked.

"Just as you wished, Mother. But there's a price for this. You are no longer my Mama," Salome said in a mocking voice. She turned and strode out of the room, leaving Herodias alone.

Stunned, Herodias glanced at the hideous sight at her feet and then turned quickly away, vomit swelling in her throat. What could she do now? What plan could be hatched to clean up this ghastly mess? Giving the head a wide berth, she headed for the door.

'I will go to my daughter. We will make this up somehow. She will call me Mama again,' Herodias thought. Unable to keep herself from once more looking at the bloody head of her enemy, Herodias turned. 'Oh, you Baptizer,' she said to herself, 'we have killed you. Will you now kill us?'

When Herodias found her daughter, Salome was standing in front of the mirror, staring at herself in horror.

'Look at her there. Oh God, she is hurt. How can she will herself back to innocence, to beauty? Can she wash off the stain of crime? I can, but can she?'

Salome gave the dark bulk of her mane a toss, went to the wash basin, and scrubbed her hands. 'I'll never tell her,' she thought. 'I'll never tell Mother what has happened to me. I'll never be the same again, and she cannot console me. Why did she push me into such a crime?' Salome looked down at her blood-spattered hands. 'Why doesn't all this blood come off?'

She rubbed her skin until it hurt, then took off her clothes and adornments and threw them against the wall. "I'll never dance again, I hate these clothes," she said aloud and, turning, saw her mother. She scowled while tears ran down her cheeks. She took a step toward Herodias, then stopped. At seventeen, Salome knew that she wanted to be different from her mother. Now for the first time, she had noticed the fear hidden behind her mother's confident demeanor. Need and disgust warred in her breast.

Herodias moved toward her. "Please . . ." said Herodias, holding out her arms to Salome.

Salome stiffened, turned away, and resumed her washing. A streak of bright red blood remained on her right arm. It did not yield to her strenuous rubbing.

"I could try to . . ." Herodias began gently.

"No. Don't touch me. You can't help me now. Everything is different for us now, Mother." Salome whirled around, nearly tripping. Quickly she straightened up. "It is too late."

"But we are all we have. We are mother and daughter," Herodias pleaded.

"We are accomplices to murder, Mama. *Murder.* And what do you plan to do with the bloody head of a prophet in your possession?"

Herodias uttered a silent prayer. 'Oh God, what have I done? She is rejecting me. I had prayed for a daughter, not a son who would be snatched away to be trained in the ways of men. You granted my prayer, oh God, and I have been faithful to the vow I made. I pledged I would always do all in my power to assure my daughter's welfare. Haven't I kept my pledge? *Haven't* I? I have done well by her. Why does she now turn me away? I can't bear it. What will I do?'

"My daughter . . . " she said, trying one more time to reach Salome.

"Don't call me 'daughter' any more. I am going away from here, far away from you, your cunning plots, and your cursed vow. I will set myself free, where I will find my innocence again. I never wanted to kill anyone!"

The ice in Salome's voice was not melted by Herodias's hot tears. 'This is not the pique of a small child threatening to run away from home,' Herodias thought. 'She means it.'

Using her most persuasive voice and her kindest look, Herodias asked, "Where will you go? You need your mother, child. Think clearly. We'll face this together. Soon this terrible day will be behind us, and everything will be as it was. There's just one small problem—the head. Help me figure out what to do with it. We need to get rid of it. Then we can forget this ever happened."

With a harsh laugh, Salome turned away from her mother. She gazed in the mirror, stroking the splotch of blood on her lower arm, pinching it between her thumb and forefinger. 'Maybe it has meaning,' she thought. 'This Baptist was supposed to be a holy man, right? Perhaps this mark is a blessing instead of a curse.'

Then Salome turned to Herodias. Her voice thick with scorn, she commanded, "Put the head in a sturdy bag and bring it here. I will take it to its owners, John's disciples. I will take it myself."

Herodias's hand flew to her chest "You can't do that. Have you gone crazy? You could get killed. Just help me bury it, that's all. Come on."

"Bring it to me," Salome repeated. "This is my task. I am the one who actually asked for the murder, remember Mother? I will make up for this, not you. I'll be all right. The Baptist preached repentance, didn't he?"

"What are you talking about, Salome? You are not in your right mind. We will talk later. Right now we have a task to do. But wait—what have you been rubbing on your arm? Let me see."

Salome hid her arm behind her back, then angrily thrust it forward at Herodias. "See? Yes. You can see. This is the blood of our victim. It's a curse on us. Our love is now pale and drained because of your ravenous ambition. Remember this blood spilled between us. Guilt blood, Mother. Now go get the bloody head!"

Herodias stood motionless. 'She was beautiful and sweet. Now my daughter is ugly and cruel. Is she possessed? I have misjudged things. She was too young for such a thing. Oh God, how will I heal my beloved daughter? How will I restore our relationship? How now will I keep my vow to take care of her?'

Helplessly, Herodias watched Salome pack. A few times she tried to make her case again, but Salome had her own ideas.

For the first time, Salome concealed her exact plans from Herodias. She brushed past her mother to retrieve the head of the Baptist, stopping for a moment to look back for one last glimpse, wondering if—and half hoping that—Herodias would run after her. Salome felt brave. And scared.

O

Carrying the head of John the Baptist in a sack slung over her shoulder and a small bag of belongings, Salome left. She left the place where she had lived for over ten years, shielded and pampered by her mother. She left the palatial grandeur below which John the Baptist had been imprisoned in a dungeon and beheaded by her stepfather, Herod Antipas. She left the spacious grounds once created by her mother's grandfather, Herod the Great, that stood nestled within a great bowl-shaped cluster of mountains, well below sea level, the city of Tiberias not far off. She left the tepid and stifling air and the pools of bubbling springs that dotted the countryside. She left the encampment atop Machaerus, the peak above the Dead Sea where Herod's army guarded the approach to Petra . . . where the fateful dance had taken place. She left, walking into the starless night, a small shadowy figure and an unlikely night trespasser in the Galilean countryside. She breathed deeply, then sucked at the still, dank air as if it could give her something. As she moved farther from the security of the royal shelter, she thought of the distance between herself and her mother, a distance she both feared and desired.

"Oh God, I am alone now. Who will keep watch over me? Will I perish because of my own foolishness, because of my mother's rash spirit? She taught me many things. The only one that seems of any use to me now is prayer. It helps, makes me feel like I have a companion, sort of. I have a burden, one she should be carrying. She didn't teach me well enough about life, so I am going to find John's people to teach me more and show me another way. For you know I am not guilty, God. This was Mama's fault. She forced me into the dance and forced me into the murder request. I tried to get out of it, but what could I do, God? There I was, standing before Herod, with all eyes on me. What choice had my mother given me? So I said it, but I said it softly. Herod's toady little henchman heard my request, though, and repeated it into Herod's ear: 'Give her the head of the Baptist, and she wants it on a platter,' he said. Why did I ask for a *platte*r? Did I think it would be neater? Oh God, I'd laugh if I could. Show me the way."

Salome set a course along the mountains' edge, eastward toward the sea. She had heard that the disciples of John roamed these hills, baptizing and making converts for a new kingdom. 'Good,' she thought. 'I hope it takes over from the wretched Herod. But how will I ever find them? Perhaps they're not that far away. Wouldn't they come to claim the headless body of their master for proper burial? Yes.'

"And I have his head," she said softly, ". . . and the mark of his blood."

○

Herodias passed that night in anguish. She prayed that God would keep her daughter from harm and bring her back safely. "It's my fault. I handled this all wrong. I should have prepared Salome for the fatal request. But how could I have done that? I wasn't sure myself until I saw that she had Herod seduced. That drunken old fox." Then the thought of Herod's ineptitude gave her hope. "Yes. Tomorrow I will petition him to set in motion a search for Salome. If he could behead his political opponent for us, surely he would do this. Yes. Tomorrow."

O

"Stupid woman! Stupid, ugly, conniving woman!" Herod pushed his face close to Herodias's. "You want me to help you get your daughter back? You used her to take advantage of me. You manipulated me into a dangerous act. The whole realm will be in an uproar over this. I was hostage to your schemes, your daughter's peril, and my chief advisor's bloodthirsty urges. I was helpless. You backed me into a corner, and I had to save face."

"Not helpless, Herod, just drunk," Herodias spat back.

"Your simpering daughter was struck dumb with terror. That's how worthless your influence is. It took my chief advisor to interpret her request. And once the crowd got a hint and their blood lust was incited, I had no control. Did you plot this, too?"

"No, Herod, I am loyal to you. I knew you were unsure about this Baptist and the way he's been rallying the people. I am on your side. Please, husband, believe me." Herodias placed her hand on Herod's shoulder, praying that God would soften his heart.

Herod's voice became a whine. "I cannot help you now, wife. I am in the middle of a campaign. You deserve nothing for your impudent intrusion into royal politics, and Salome deserves to perish after her shameless exhibition. I will not risk my legions to go out after a lone girl, probably by now devoured in the wilds or set on by a band of robbers. She should never have left your side. You should never have let her go. And your vow to protect her? The reason you persuaded me to marry you in the first place—to protect your interests? Ha! As good as water through a sieve. Get out of here. I will not help you or your daughter."

Herodias watched as Herod strode away. She went back to her chambers where she crumpled onto her bed. There she stayed, limp with grief, day after day, wrapped in a gloom so impenetrable that eventually only her maidservant, Chloe, remained in attendance.

"Do you remember," Chloe would whisper into Herodias's ear as she tenderly bathed her, "do you remember when Salome and I got lost in the dungeon area where we weren't allowed to go? We were so scared, but Salome said you would save us. You did . . . and you never told on us either. Remember? You used to love to watch us laugh and play. You are smart and strong still, just like you always were. We will find Salome. And I am praying all the time. I just know Salome will be all right with my father's people."

Chloe wrapped a warm, damp cloth around Herodias's feet and washed them with care. Chloe could feel a gradual relaxing of Herodias's stiff muscles as she massaged fragrant oils into the skin of her feet and legs, her arms and hands, her neck and shoulders, working up to the worn, dry skin of her face, streaked with tears. Herodias said nothing and did not seem to hear Chloe's chatter.

"You remember my father, don't you?" Chloe went on. "I used to tell Salome about his faith and his people and their hopes for a messiah who would change the world, make things just and peaceful. Salome loved to listen. Did she ever tell you about it? We used to play kingdom games. Salome wanted to be the ruler, but she let me have a turn at it sometimes."

Herodias shifted her head to look at Chloe. Spurred by this small response, Chloe continued. "Yes, I bet Salome right now is safe with my father. He is kind and good. His people are, too, and will probably remind Salome of her devotion to her mother. I am praying for that, anyway. And one day I will hear from my father. Every few months he gets word to us."

"When?"

Herodias's one word startled Chloe. "Did you say something?"

"When?" Herodias repeated, her raspy voice just above a whisper.

"When? Oh, I don't know. Speak more to me. It isn't good to be so silent and alone in your own mind. No one has been to see you for months now, and you go nowhere. You don't even talk! You don't want Salome to find you in this condition when she returns, do you? Can't you at least get angry? You always did that a lot. 'Here comes Mama's storm,' Salome would warn, and we would run and hide."

Herodias laughed, a gurgle from her throat.

"Did you laugh? Is that you laughing?"

Herodias laughed and sobbed all at once. Chloe placed her hand behind her mistress's back and lifted her up in the bed. She held Herodias's shaking body until the trembling subsided.

"Salome said that? She said 'Mama's storm'?" Herodias laughed, her eyes brightening. "What a girl, my girl. She knew me well, she loved me, until . . ."

"No. Don't fall silent again." Chloe shook Herodias's shoulder.

Herodias stared at Chloe.

"You have been so sick, even feverish. It's not good for

you to sink down into your sadness." Chloe looked into Herodias's eyes, again gone blank. "I will return soon with supper. A good hot soup will bring the color back to your face."

○

Salome stumbled along over miles of uneven and rocky terrain, dotted with brush and thistle. She could find little food and water. Her clothes were tattered. "I can't bear it another moment. How many days has it been? Oh God, I will die out here. There is nothing to eat. I will die," she cried out. "It would be easier if I could just leave this head behind. It's so heavy. Why do I lug this thing? What good will it do me? Oh, I can't walk another step." She collapsed, exhausted, onto the hard ground. "I don't care if I die. I don't care. I don't care." She tapped at the bloodstain on her arm and closed her eyes.

The passage of time meant nothing to Salome as she lay there waiting to die, drifting in and out of consciousness. Gradually, a delicious wetness broke through her stupor. It touched her lips. It drew her life up and up, into her throat, her mouth, her lips. She sucked at the water with all the strength she had left.

○

That night, as Chloe stood in the kitchen preparing dinner for Herodias, hoping again that it would revive her spirits, she heard a scratching near the door to the lower courtyard where the palace servants came and went from the kitchen to their basement quarters. It was so faint she ignored it at first, but it kept up. Finally she opened the door a crack to see whether an animal was making the noise, but she saw nothing and went back to her work at the sink. The sound came again. Chloe felt the hair on her forearms rise and her skin tingle. What could this be?

She opened the door again and called loudly, "Who is there? We admit no one to these rooms after dusk." The light was waning and shadows moved in the courtyard, but all else was still. "Must be my imagination," she muttered.

"Chloe?"

Chloe turned quickly, scanning the yard. She saw nothing.

"Chloe," the voice said, a little louder.

"Is that you, Papa? It sounds like you."

"Around the corner by the swine slops. Come."

Chloe found her father crouching behind a corn crib. She knelt down, and he pulled her close. "Sh-h-h." he said, placing his forefinger on her lips. She nodded.

"Listen carefully, my child. They have found your friend Salome. She was half-dead from exposure and deprivation. It is very dangerous in the land. The Baptist's people are growing in numbers. They go about saying this Jesus is the messiah. He is preaching a new reign. This is what I have waited and prayed for."

"Papa, your dream, the vision of your people. Is it true?"

"I don't know. All I know is that Herod is threatened and all of us following Jesus are in danger for disturbing the peace of the land. Conflict with the ruling authorities could mean . . ."

"Oh no, Papa. You should not be in these groups. You are not safe with your own people now, and you're not safe here either. But what is he like, this Jesus? Surely he will punish Salome for the murder of his friend . . . my God, I never thought of that before. You told me your people are good. Are they good enough to forgive murder?"

"They are. Don't worry. Jesus is in charge. He is not vengeful. He is the strangest man I have ever met, such a mixture of passions, fierce and furious, about his message, his God, but soft and almost powerless when he talks to all of us who gather. He doesn't seem to want to stir an uprising, has no interest in claiming the land. Strange. Oh, and he laughs a lot, too, even in the midst of our dire conditions, but his laugh is compassionate, soothing in a way."

Chloe had never seen her father look like this, almost hypnotized as he talked about Jesus. She felt calm listening to him talk. She settled into his arms as they observed together the passing of the day, the onset of evening. 'Oh God,' she whispered inside herself. 'Please let it all be true.'

"Papa, I must go now. I have to take Herodias her meal. I'm worried about her. Will you hug my friend Salome for me, Papa? When will it be safe for us to be together? Will Jesus make it safe for us all? I miss you so much."

"Hush, child. I know. I want the same thing. We will pray."

○

The followers of John the Baptist had taken Salome back to their camp where, after several days, she had regained her strength, aided by the ministrations of Chloe's father.

"Why did you kill him?" the leaders of the Baptist's group asked her.

"I didn't," she said.

"You didn't? You carried his head. What better evidence?"

"But I didn't! It was Herod . . . and my mother's idea. I saved his head to bring to you."

The interrogations went on for days until Salome wept in exhaustion. Finally, Chloe's father persuaded them to let her live on the edge of the camp. "She is a child," he said, "a child. Leave her now. What good is more hostility and pain? This is not our way."

Salome and Chloe's father spoke little, except when she thanked him for his care.

"Salome, what is that stain on your arm?" he asked her one day.

"Oh, have I thanked you for saving me and for taking care of me until I could move without pain? Have I?"

"Yes, child, many times."

"You know I always envied Chloe. My father never came to see me after Mama left him to marry Herod. Do you remember when you would come to visit, and I would ask you all those questions about your people, your faith?"

Chloe's father nodded. "Once you told me I had chosen God over Chloe. You said it wasn't fair."

"It wasn't. What did you answer?"

Chloe's father laughed. "I don't remember. I think I defended God. But you have not answered me. What is the stain you carry on your arm?"

"I'm not sure. Well, I know it is the blood of John the Baptist, but I don't know why it doesn't come off. I've scrubbed and scrubbed. Maybe it's a curse . . . maybe it's a blessing. I don't know what it means, do you?"

"No."

"You and your people and Jesus talk about forgiveness a lot. Why is that?"

"If people hurt you, or you hurt them, it makes a stain on your soul. Forgiveness cancels the debt of an injury so you are free, free not to worry and wrestle about it any more. It's a kind of healing . . . not like the hurt never happened, but that it is not going to take over your life, your thoughts, your feelings all the time. Forgiveness lets the one who hurt you stop hurting you over and over in your mind."

Salome was silent. She looked at the bloodstain and brushed her hand over it lightly.

"I know your Jesus says God forgives. Do you think I am good enough for that? I did bring you John's head, after all. That must count for something. I could have left it to rot in the mountains."

Chloe's father nodded. He did not tell Salome about the community's resentment. Only with reluctance had they decided to let her travel with them rather than leave her to perish. They treated her with care but no affection—except for Chloe's father, who suspected there was more to the story than what was assumed.

"Maybe Jesus will be nice. Maybe he will teach me your ways and about forgiveness. Maybe . . ." Salome said.

"Do you feel guilty, Salome?" Chloe's father asked.

"Yes and no. It wasn't my fault exactly. But I guess it is always good to have forgiveness from God when a life is taken and you are involved, even if it wasn't exactly your fault. Don't you think?"

Salome did not ask if God would forgive her mother.

○

Over the next months, Salome prayed and sang with the community. She listened and learned and watched for Jesus to notice her. But he didn't.

'Well, I guess I will have to talk to him, then,' she said to herself. She circled around the edge of the camp to where Jesus sat. As she went, a woman spat at her, and another put her arm on the first one's shoulder and frowned.

"Hello," Salome said.

Jesus didn't look up at her.

'Oh, he's praying. I'm interrupting him.' She turned to go.

"Did you want to speak to me, Salome?" Jesus asked.

The panic Salome felt was akin to what she had felt in front of Herod, but it melted when she saw the peaceful look on Jesus' face. "I thought you could tell me more about your ideas . . . or about my mother . . . or something."

"What do you want?"

"Well, I want . . . "

Jesus waited.

Salome ran her toe round in the sand, circling one way and then the other. 'Why doesn't he say something?' she wondered, rubbing her hands together.

Jesus smiled. Then he laughed and reached out to her.

With her hands in his, she said, "I want Mama, Mama. No, I don't really. I'm mad at her. She hurt me and I've left her."

"What do you want, then?"

Salome's tears flowed. Jesus drew her to his breast and held her there while she sobbed, "I want . . . I want . . ."

He stroked her hair and breathed soothing words she didn't understand. When she felt calmer, she began to fall asleep in his arms. He drew up a blanket and placed her on it, kissing her tenderly on the cheek and bidding her sleep without fear.

○

As she brought Herodias her dinner, Chloe moved to prop up Herodias from where she had again slumped down on her pillows. "I have something to tell you."

"Go away now. I'm better alone."

"No. Listen. My father came. They have found Salome. She is alive. Rescued."

Herodias said nothing.

"Did you hear? Your daughter is alive and well. She is with my father's people."

Chloe watched as light began to creep into Herodias's eyes and blush onto her face. She sat up slowly. "Is this true? Do not deceive me, girl."

"Yes, it is true. Yes. Yes."

The news sliced through Herodias. "No more of this futile praying, lying around, then. I will send for my daughter." Herodias spoke sharply as she roused herself. "Get me my robes, girl. Quickly. I will go to the king."

"Maybe it would be better to wait until morning. Maybe you should think through what you want to do," Chloe said.

Herodias stood unsteadily on her feet, listing to one side as she groped for her robes. "No. I must go now." She waved Chloe aside and left the room, gaining strength with each step. She went toward Herod's chamber, ready to beg. "Yes, that's what I'll have to do . . . beg . . . how disgusting!" she muttered to herself.

○

"What do you want with me at this hour of night, wife?"

"Salome is safe. Chloe heard it in the market. She has been found by the followers of the Baptist, and the new one, Jesus. You are powerful, my dear husband." Herodias sat on the bed where Herod rested. "I know you can do anything. Let us send for Salome tomorrow. You with all your resources can discover her whereabouts. She must be returned to her beloved mother, and . . ."

Herod's silence scoffed at Herodias.

". . . and to you, the only father she really knows. You have always treated her as your own. I know she loves you, Herod . . ."

"She is cursed by the Baptist's blood. The people will turn against me even more. On the other hand, perhaps I could make it a peace offering, tell them I intended to punish Salome severely for her crime and for setting a trap for me. They will want revenge, of course. This could serve me well."

"Yes. Yes. That is sound thinking, Herod, a good plan, a very good plan." Herodias bent forward to kiss Herod who seized her, fumbling at her breasts. "Yes, dear wife. I will have you tonight. And tomorrow you will have your daughter."

'And tomorrow I will have my daughter,' Herodias said to herself with joy. 'Tomorrow I will make a plan to save Salome from Herod's punitive plan. Tomorrow I will again be loyal to my vow.'

But tomorrow came and went, and Herodias did not have her daughter. She had not counted on Salome's refusal to return home.

Herod's messenger had found the camp. He offered peace and told of his errand. He waited at the edges of their camp, fearing for his life. After a while Chloe's father came to greet the messenger.

"The girl Salome will not come with you."

"But her mother . . ."

"She says to tell her mother that she will not return and that if she is captured by force, she will close her heart forever. Go and tell your mistress."

○

Herodias was driven near mad by her daughter's refusal to come home, but she was wise enough to know she could not force Salome, not again. "This is the Baptist's revenge," she snarled to herself.

"*It is your own,*" said God-in-Herodias.

Herodias looked around her room. "Who is here?" She looked in the mirror and saw her own reflection. "I am here," she said and walked closer to the mirror, shedding her robe as she went and watching a solo tear roll down her ashen cheek.

Herodias had never looked at herself much before, but now she stared intently at her own pain. "Is it I who speaks or does God speak to me? Who is this powerless woman before me? Who is this who weeps for herself? Oh God, how I long for you, for someone to love me. The one beloved I vowed myself to protect now hates me and is gone." She placed her hand gently against the mirror's glass and stroked the reflection of her face, which softened to her touch.

"*It is not the vow—not its making, not its breaking. It's that you loved the vow more than you loved your daughter.*"

Herodias jumped back. "Is that you?" Only silence answered her. "What daughter will I love now, oh God? Who?"

○

Over the next two years Herodias and Salome had no contact save for the considerable spiritual energy that traveled the miles between them in their thoughts and prayers.

Over time, Herodias experienced a gradual change of heart. It had begun that day in front of the mirror when she had heard the truth. 'I suppose that was from God,' Herodias thought, 'because if it weren't from God, I wouldn't be feeling so much better, in spite of the pain of losing Salome.'

"You know, Chloe," Herodias said one day, "I have come to respect Salome for leaving me. Can you believe that?"

Chloe nodded.

Herodias went on, smiling. "Defiance rather becomes her. But it does not become me, not at all, to defy God's law of love for a vow I couldn't keep anyway. Love is not a vow, you know."

Chloe, who had listened to Herodias talk so much about her precious vow, sighed with relief.

"Chloe, I did wrong by my daughter. I know that now. Oh God, I know that now. But I can't change what I did, so I will have to live with my heartache until I die."

"But . . ." Chloe began.

"No. Don't try to dissuade me. You know I am right. Salome at least is alive and perhaps will have a better life now, but not much luxury. Ah well. That should be enough. But I need to take some kind of action, something to show I have changed. Something to prove to myself, to prove it . . ."

"To Salome?" Chloe asked.

"I'd like that, but no. Salome does not need to know what I do. I guess I need something to show God. Does that sound silly to you, Chloe? You are the religious one, you and your good father."

"It's not silly." Chloe smiled at her mistress.

"But what? What will I do? I'll have to think about this."

Soon an unexpected opportunity came. Herod asked Herodias to sit at his side for an upcoming hearing. At first she declined, thinking it would be another foolish contest of wills, but when she found out that the man to be tried was Jesus, she changed her mind.

"It will be amusing, my dear," Herod said. "A chance to see a madman defend himself. He's trying to start a revolution, and we can't have that."

Herodias immediately thought of Salome's safety. She wanted no revolution.

Herod continued. "Pilate, the Roman governor has found no reason for a trial against this man Jesus, but the people are stirred up. I am curious. Perhaps we will close the chapter John the Baptist started, once and for all. What do you think?"

Herodias shook inside at the thought and the memory. But she straightened her spine and said, "What has this to do with the Baptist? Is there danger, my husband?"

"Foolish woman, your crime comes back to haunt you," Herod laughed.

The day of the hearing dawned hot, so hot the air stuck in Herodias's throat as she sat next to Herod. "Herod," she whispered, "remember that this Jesus is one of the group that Salome has traveled with."

Herod shrugged and brushed her arm away.

Herodias felt perspiration on her brow. Now she would finally see this man she had heard so much about. Perhaps she could do something to influence the turn of events. Perhaps she would even see her daughter in the crowd.

The confrontation proceeded in the usual way: Herod

toyed with Jesus like a cat with a mouse. But Jesus did not respond to the bait.

"Herod, look at him," Herodias whispered. "Look how he is not afraid. See how he stands? I don't like it that he does nothing to defend himself. It wouldn't take much to make his case. Saying that you are one with God isn't the same as saying you are God. Why doesn't Jesus speak up? Herod, do you hear me?"

"Shut up, Herodias. My interrogation is just beginning."

Herod questioned and mocked and demanded evidence. Herodias could see he was getting nowhere. She put her hand again on the sleeve of his garment. This time he turned to her.

"What will we do?" he asked. "People are at the brink of riot, Jesus' fans adore him, and the religious leaders want him sentenced for blasphemy."

"Your mind is muddled, husband." Herodias squeezed his arm. "You do not want his blood, as well as that of John the Baptist, on your hands. You have nothing to stand on except your own pride. Send him back to Pilate. Let the Roman law make the decision." She could feel Herod's breath release, his arm relax. He would do as she suggested.

Herodias sat back in her seat and smiled. She could barely keep from jumping for joy. 'This is it! I've acted and succeeded. Jesus will be spared. Pilate will not want to deal with this insurrection, ruthless as he is. He already tried to pass it off on us, didn't he? Oh God, thank you. Perhaps I have been part of saving Jesus' life, avenging the Baptist's blood. The people love Jesus. He is a hero. Surely, even if it goes to the point of sentence, the people will choose another criminal for execution, and Pilate will have to set Jesus free. I've done it! I've made things better for Salome, for Jesus . . . and yes, for me.'

○

When the news came about the transfer of Jesus back to Pilate, many thought it could spare his life. But just as many were skeptical about the brutal politics of the Roman state.

"I'm not too worried, are you?" Salome said to Chloe's father. "I mean, about Jesus. After all, he's innocent. He doesn't even need God's forgiveness. Not like me."

"Not like you?" Chloe's father asked. "Of what are you guilty, Salome?"

"Well, at first I thought I was guilty of murder, but that was a trap," Salome told him. "Now I think I'm guilty of blaming my mother for the whole thing, of not seeing it from her side. She was scared, and she had vowed to protect me. It was her way of showing her love, even if it was desperate."

"So you have forgiven your mother?" Chloe's father asked, smiling.

"I think I have," said Salome. "Yes, I think I have. I can tell by how I feel when I think of her."

"How is that?"

"It sounds silly, but I feel, well, almost proud. My mother really tried hard, very hard, with her whole heart, to make everything right for me. So I forgive her. I can say 'Mama' without feeling contempt, and I can pray we will see each other again."

"That's how you know?

Salome nodded. "And one more thing. Jesus told me about the God-in-me voice that speaks wisdom. He said to listen for it. So I did, and one day my God-in-Salome voice told me I wasn't as innocent as I thought. And I believed it."

Chloe's father gave Salome a hug, then left her sitting on a rock at the edge of the camp.

Salome sat for some time and gazed at the distant hills. She was rubbing her arm where the bloodstain had remained, not even noticing that it was gone. She thought about Jesus and her mother. "I'm worried about Jesus, God," she prayed. "But I know he has your voice in him, too. All the same, please let him be safe."

Her worried prayers dwindled into silence, a silence so profound she could not even hear her own heart beat, a silence that wrapped itself around her like a cloak, a silence that soothed. In the midst of that silence, Salome knew something else. She knew that the decision to transfer Jesus to Pilate had been her mother's action, her mother's advice to Herod. She knew Herod would never have thought of this on his own. She knew it because she knew her mother. She *knew* her mother.

"Oh, Mama," she said aloud, getting up from her seat on the rock. "Oh, Mama, a good work. One day I will thank you in person. Mama, Mama."

Considerations for Prayer and Reflection

"What you did not dare in your life you dare in mine."

Marge Piercy, "My Mother's Body,"
THE ART OF BLESSING THE DAY: POEMS WITH A JEWISH THEME

For personal prayer:

Following the guidelines for prayer described on page 16, reflect first on what the God Between might be doing between you and this midrash text:

- What got your attention?
- What brought a reaction, either positive or negative?
- Where did you feel the *hum* of the story in you?
- What relationship is the God-in-you calling you to explore through the story's characters or events?

For reflection:

Sometimes—actually, quite often—mothers and daughters fight. Like Herodias and Salome, we hurt each other as we strive to be selves in a girdle of closeness that threatens to subsume individuality. Mothers can burst with pride in their daughters and shrivel with fear, all at once. Daughters can bask in their mother's attention and seethe with freedom's call, all at once.

I can imagine a mother and daughter like Herodias and Salome coming for relationship counseling after a long period of estrangement and disconnection. Both long for a new and tension-free connection; both feel misunderstood. Each needs desperately to ask hard questions of the other; and each is desirous but fearful of telling the other her true story, fearful of hearing the other's true story.

God spends all of God's good time listening to the

prayers of the people of the world. It is by doing the same thing that we will bring about the ways of divine love in our world. It is so simple and so not easy. We want all the time to use our one mouth instead of our two ears.

Herodias and Salome had to experience distance, both emotionally and geographically, in order to tune into the God Between in themselves and in the space between them. Their growth and healing happened apart, and it happened because they listened to others around them and also to the sounds of sheer silence in their personal solitudes. Out of those kinds of solitudes, memories are harvested and healing wisdom comes.

The modern mother and daughter would have done the same thing already or they wouldn't be sitting in my office, looking tentatively at each other and using up a whole box of tissues as they listened to the sound of each other's voices, finally emerging out of each one's silence.

For further consideration on your own or in a group:

- How do you see the healing role of the God Between in the relationship between Herodias and Salome?

- In your mind what might a reunion between Herodias and Salome have been like?

- Have you ever made a well-intentioned parenting vow and had it backfire?

- As an adult, what kind of relationship do you have with your mother? Your adult child?

- What has your experience of forgiveness been? Is there someone you need to forgive now?

The Final Petition

QUEEN ESTHER AND A PALACE EUNUCH

(The Book of Esther)

○

How can a deeply connected friendship be life-saving?

○

Hathach's slender brown arm shot out from behind the pillar and stopped Esther's fall. For a brief moment, their eyes met, his from a shadowy hiding place, hers reflected in the mirror accuracy of polished shell and onyx floors. His sharp glance compelled her; her astounding beauty held him in its spell.

Their connection was quickly broken by the force of the king's eunuch, Hegai. Taking a firm hold on Esther's arm, he brought her back in line with the other maidens he was herding into the harem.

Esther reluctantly broke her gaze with Hathach, wondering, 'Who is this lovely, brown man with the fierce stare? I wonder if I will see more of him?'

'Who is this bright woman?' Hathach mused. 'She looks different from the rest, small like a child. Who will teach her the palace ways?'

Their mutual curiosity would not be satisfied for several days.

In the women's quarters, Hegai addressed the women:

"I am Hegai, the king's eunuch. You are gathered here as an honor, eight of the most beautiful virgins, all the king's favorite kind of good looks. One lucky one of you will be crowned queen in a year." He looked around, inspecting each face. Esther shivered when he came to her. "Are you all listening to me carefully? I will only repeat these instructions once. Once."

The young women stood still in silence. They nodded.

"All right, then, I will begin," he continued. "First, you are not to leave these premises or your own quarters without permission. You are not to keep company with any of the palace servants, although each of you will have a personal attendant to help you with preparations. For six months your bodies will be lavished with special oils, and for another six months with perfumes and cosmetics. All the attendants are eunuchs. Do you know what a eunuch is? A eunuch is a useless man, a non-man." Hegai laughed dryly. "Eunuchs don't care about the likes of you. But the king does."

'We are being fattened up for the slaughter,' Esther thought. 'Oh God, why am I here?'

Noticing her grimace, Hegai stepped over to Esther and gave her a sharp look. Esther stood a little straighter and found the courage to address him: "When will each of us know who her attendant is? Do we get a choice?"

Acting as if he had not even heard her question, Hegai continued. "As I was saying, one of you will be the new queen. You have undoubtedly heard of the fate of the former queen, Vashti. She refused the king, sinned by denying her husband. Now she is dethroned and banished." He paused again, squinting at the small group of women. "How wonderful to be queen, hmmm? Only one, just one of you. The rest of you will remain here in service for the rest of your lives, to come only when summoned. You will be part of the king's harem, a kind of royalty . . . but not quite. Not quite." Hegai gazed meaningfully at each terrified young face and then abruptly left the room.

Esther turned her head slightly to glance at the maidens nearest her. One had tears flowing down her cheeks, another had turned ghostly pale. Esther's own fists were clenched. 'What an arrogant idiot,' she thought. 'I hope my eunuch is the one I saw in the hall. I hope I'll meet him soon. Could he be friendly? This is a dangerous place for me—a contender for queen and a Jew. Oh God, a Jewish girl in the Persian palace! What was Mordecai *thinking* when he brought me here?'

○

"Do you like the aroma of the oils?" Hathach inquired, after handing her a new set of clothing. Through a bit of palace maneuvering, he had, in fact, arranged to become Esther's attendant.

"We do have the best fragrances," Esther said. "Why do you smile so? Are you, my attendant, flirting with me perhaps?" Even as these words had tumbled out, Esther worried she had been too bold. 'I don't even know this man, let alone if I can trust him. I'm always doing things like this.'

But Hathach only enjoyed her playfulness and asked how she had come to be a contender for the queen's throne.

"My cousin Mor . . . my cousin, sent me here." Thoughts of Mordecai brought tears to Esther's eyes.

Hathach leaned slightly toward Esther. "Are you crying?"

"No," Esther answered. "No, I just had a thought."

"A thought of what?" Hathach asked.

"It's not important," Esther said, turning away.

"I suppose your cousin had your best interest in mind. This could be an honor, a great honor indeed. Don't you agree?"

Esther shrugged.

"You do not agree then?" Hathach smiled down at her.

Esther lowered her eyes and thought, 'He mocks me. I wish this eunuch could be my friend, but he doesn't understand my plight. An honor, he says!'

Hathach watched Esther's tentative steps as she left to put the clothing in her dressing room. His heart flooded with sorrow for this young, innocent girl. Tears came as he remembered the first day that, as a young boy, he been brought to this palace. He trembled, seeing in his mind's eye the glint of the descending blade.

When Esther returned, she sat down and placed her hand on Hathach's arm. "I don't even know your name yet. I am Esther."

"My name is Hathach," he said, looking down at his arm.

"What will it be like when I am finally brought before the king, Hathach?" Esther asked with a worried look.

"You will probably be selected first. I have looked around carefully at the other young women, and I have a discerning eye," Hathach said without a smile. "You will then be declared queen and officially belong to King Ahasueras as the first wife."

Esther said nothing.

"Don't worry . . . it must be every maiden's dream." Hathach smiled.

"It doesn't seem quite so easy to me," Esther replied. "This will be an ordeal. Cosmetics, fragrances, crowns! I am not like all the others; this is not my dream come true. You know nothing about me, so don't make assumptions. I hate kings. I especially hate *fat* kings. And I am to serve no one but the God of my . . ."

Esther caught herself as Hathach stared at her.

Silently, she considered: 'We are both sold into slavery, Hathach and I. He as a eunuch, I as a woman of the harem. Just as my people were. Oh God, let this man be a friend. Help me take this risk.'

Esther looked up at Hathach. "Hegai said eunuchs weren't even men. He is wrong. Hathach, you *are* a man. You are a kind man. Will you help me, teach me the inside palace ways, I . . ."

Hathach put his hand up to hush her. He had never met a woman of such audacity. 'Except for Vashti,' he thought. 'And look what happened to her . . . '

"I must go now," he said aloud and walked off, leaving Esther alone.

'I am a fool,' Esther thought as she returned to her chamber and fell onto her bed. The linens were white, of the finest fabric, trimmed with cords of purple and gold. Esther rubbed her cheek against the softness.

'Why did I let my thoughts come out raw like that? Now I have lost the chance to have a friend. Oh merciful Lord God, help me now. I don't want to be a queen. The king looks old enough to be my father. Oh Papa, Papa, why aren't you here? None of this would have happened to me if you were here. Why did you and Mama die? Mordecai is not you! This palace ordeal is to satisfy him, not me. He said it was for me, but it's for *him*, isn't it Papa? Isn't it, God?' Esther moved from the bed to the couch and stroked its plush green satin. 'I must think. I must survive. You will have to be my friend, God. Make me smart. Show me a way.'

O

'She said I was a man,' Hathach thought. He hadn't thought so much in a long time. 'I want to help her, but it's against the rules. I'm only a eunuch. But she said I was a *man*. I feel warm and my skin tingles. If I didn't know better, I'd wonder if I was in fact a eunuch. No, I am a man. I will help her.'

Three days later, when Hathach found Esther sitting alone, he announced, "I've decided to help you."

"Why?" she asked.

"What does it matter why? You say you are different. You speak of God. I don't know about God anymore, but I will tell you that ten years ago I was forced into this service just as you were. Not my dream either. But my situation is a worse trap than yours."

"Worse? *Worse*, you say, Hathach? What's worse? We are both trapped and exploited." Esther sat up straight. "We can't just compare predicaments and decide who is worse off. If we're going to be friends, we just need to understand each other."

Hathach nodded and sat down on the floor with his legs crossed. "Tell me, about yourself, Esther."

"I will tell you." She said a brief prayer and began: "I am Jewish. I serve one God. To be chosen of God isn't much of an honor either because being Jewish is dangerous, but I'd rather have it than be queen. Sometimes we get tempted into arrogance and pride about privilege, even about our suffering. But, what's really sacred, Hathach, what's really sacred about Jews is that we are bearers of hope. Oh, we wish for a lot of things and kvetch all the time, but in our covenant we return and put our trust in the God who claims us forever. We always come back, even when things are the worst, the worst! And so, by the way, does God."

Hathach stared at her, amazed.

"So you see, I want to be faithful to the covenant. I want to do something . . . I just don't know what. I had dreamed of being a powerful actor in the drama of divine salvation. Me, a woman. Ha! But we do have women heroes of the faith, and I wanted to be one. But now I am sold into slavery, like the Israelites in Egypt. Will God deliver me too?"

"I . . ." Hathach reached out to touch Esther's hand then drew back. "I will . . ."

"Save me? Deliver me?" Esther laughed.

"Don't laugh at me," he said sharply.

"No, Hathach. I don't laugh at you. I know you are good. I just feel so helpless, alone here with no people, no family."

"I have read your people's stories. You must have hope, just as you say. Esther, you are a faithful woman, but I fear for you. Don't reveal your identity here in the palace. Have you heard talk of Haman, the grand vizier? He is wicked. He hates Jews and . . ."

"My identity as a Jew is all I have now," Esther protested.

"Yes, and you will still have it. It's branded into your soul. Just don't talk about it."

"What good is that?"

"You will see," Hathach said. "But for now let me tell you what to expect. And let me tell you of Queen Vashti. She was like you: She was honest, but she could speak rashly. Let me help you find your way in the court. Perhaps you will fulfill more of your dream here than you imagine. But first you need to become queen. Who knows what this God of yours can do?"

○

The months passed, and Hathach did as he promised, telling Esther all he knew about what was going on in the courts. He coached Esther in what the king hoped for in his next queen, reminding her that if she were to have any power at all, she must first secure the royal favor. They grew clever at non-verbal signals and secret ways to meet. Strengthened by a growing trust, Esther and Hathach became good friends. By the time the important day arrived, Esther was prepared.

Hathach watched as Esther paraded with the maidens before the king, each bowing as she approached. As Hathach watched Esther's well-rehearsed moves, his thoughts moved with her. 'She is poised. Good. Don't smile, Esther. Yes, that's it. We have worked out this process well. The king is paying attention. Your beauty makes you a sure bet!'

King Ahasueras sat on his massive throne, swathed in ermine-trimmed robes. The walls of the throne room were inlaid with pearls and precious stones, and hung with white and gold linen embroideries. Couches of gold and silver bordered with gold braid stood near the throne.

As Esther bowed before him, the king leaned forward. Hathach held his breath. Esther kept her head lowered, looking modest, humble, as planned. Hathach almost laughed at her excellent performance.

The king arose and walked over to Esther. He circled her, stared as if measuring and staking out a piece of choice land. Then he returned to his throne, reached over and picked up the crown.

'Will it be me? Yes, it looks as if he has decided . . .' Esther thought, keeping a solemn face.

Hathach's heart thumped as the king went over to Esther and placed the crown on her small head.

'I have won,' she thought, with relief. But the weight of the bejeweled crown reminded her that a new, precarious —even dangerous—existence had just begun for her.

"My queen. Queen Esther," Ahasueras shouted. "I declare amnesty and gifts in all the realm. And a great banquet in her honor!"

○

Later Queen Esther stood alone in her private quarters. "Oh God," she prayed, "help me survive this ordeal. Let me know if my submission to the king will serve some larger purpose. The king is ugly and obese. How can I endure being taken by him as his wife and lover? Show me a sign, God." Esther began to pace. She longed for Hathach's gentle talk and his cool hand on her shoulder. 'Of course,' she thought, 'Hathach can't come to me now. I am queen. But wait . . . that means that I have the power to summon him. I will!'

"Are you all right?" Hathach asked when he arrived.

"No," she said. "I am not all right." She fell tearfully against his strong body. He held her and stroked her hair until she stopped shaking.

"Hathach," she whispered. "I don't want the king's love. What can I do?"

"Esther, I think it will help if you can remember you are not powerless in all this. There are some things you can do to earn the king's favor and gain some advantage. Do you remember what I told you about the king's advisor, Haman?"

She nodded.

"He is very eager to curry the king's favor, and I have an idea about how you can help him—and yourself at the same time. I have heard rumors that there is a plot to kill the king. Tell Haman of the plot, encouraging him to be a hero as the king's informant. We need Haman on our side to break into the palace power base. He will bask in the king's favor, and Ahasueras, too, will be distracted for a time."

"Hathach, you're a genius. I love you. You are almost as clever as I am." Esther laughed with delight.

"I *am* as clever as you are, Esther. I did not tell you this before . . . because I was afraid, but I tell you now: I, too, am Jewish."

Esther gasped.

"It is a source of huge pain to me, for ten years ago when I was made a eunuch, I was excommunicated from the covenant."

"What? Is that one of the rules?"

Hathach nodded.

"Our people are not always just," Esther said. "This is an outrage."

"Esther, we have other things to plan now. This isn't important," Hathach said.

"Not important? Not *important*! For God's sake, it is very important, Hathach. You are a man, a Jewish man. As you told me, identity is an inner thing, branded on your soul. I know and God knows that you are a Jewish man. So pray like one."

"I haven't prayed in years, and I don't dare to now."

"How old are you, Hathach?" Esther sat down on the settee and looked up at him.

"Esther, what difference does that make?" Hathach scowled at her.

"How old?" she persisted.

"Twenty-four," he muttered.

Esther stared up at him with glistening eyes. "Hathach,

you were so young, a child when they . . . I am seventeen now, just three years older than you when you lost . . . and to be shunned by your people . . . my people."

"But you do not shun me, Esther," Hathach said. "You cry for me."

"Oh, Hathach, tell me about yourself. We have shared so much, but I know so little about you, except what I can see in your face. I, too, have a discerning eye."

"But, Esther, we have to make other plans."

"Plans can wait. We have all night and three days before the banquet Ahasueras will have for me . . . and my . . . my time with him. You are more important now. Tell me of yourself, Hathach. Sit here. Besides, I am queen now, and you have to obey me."

Hathach bent deeply before her. "I do as you command."

"It is good to see you smile, Hathach. Good."

He knelt in front of Esther and began. "Even after all these years, I can still feel the pain of that knife."

Esther motioned to him with a quick wave of her hand. "Hathach, we are friends, not queen and servant. Don't kneel before me. Come, sit beside me."

With clenched fists drumming his knees, Hathach joined her and continued. "I was cut, cut off. That's what my name means: *hatkuhu*, cut down. I can still smell the ointment they used to clean my wounds. I fainted. The pain of my body is not foremost now, though. More painful is my position here . . . and knowing that it was my mother who sold me to this fate for money."

"Your mother! Oh, Hathach . . . "

"Yes." Hathach bent his head very low, and Esther

reached to place her hand on his shoulder.

"Oh my God, what torture for your soul."

"And the loss of my heritage, my people. I cannot be Jewish like you." Hathach wept openly. "I'm sorry to cry, but when I tell you and you listen, it seems fresh, like a brand-new hurt."

Esther cried with him, pressing her fingers into his arm. "Your tears are important. We'll help each other because we share tears," she said. "But Hathach, if you ever get away from here, will you seek revenge? Is your mother still alive?"

"She is. My father had been dead a long time, and I know she needed money so badly, but . . . but I will never get out of here, so your question doesn't matter. I have no power."

"But *I* do," Esther said.

"We will need your power for other things, I think, Esther. But now that you know this about me, it's as if you help me carry this burden. Thank you. Is there something I can do for you in return? Are you carrying a burden that is too heavy to bear alone?"

Esther drew in a deep breath. "My cousin Mordecai . . ." she began. Esther paused before continuing, surprised at how much the story still hurt. "He adopted me when my parents died. I was a girl of eight. I was grateful for his care and the things he taught me. He is a leader of our people, and I learned much from him. I missed my mother and father terribly. I still . . ."

Hathach put his arm on hers. "Esther, what did Mordecai do?"

"Nothing really. That's why this is so silly."

"Silly? No." Hathach leaned forward to look into her tear-filled eyes.

Esther stared at Hathach for a long time, peering into his eyes that did not waver from her face. "Hathach, I feel ashamed of my feelings."

Hathach waited.

"I shouldn't be mad at Mordecai. He has the interests of my people, our people, in mind. He even coached me on how to use my feminine wiles to survive and to have power. 'You'll be queen,' he said with a great laugh. My being here does give me some clout, and I suppose that's good . . . " Esther looked aside.

"But . . . "

"But it's not for *my* good, it's for Mordecai's. He wants the power, *he's* the ambitious one. He talked me into this. I thought I'd be the hero I always wanted to be. But I don't feel like a hero at all—just a fool."

"And a sacrificial lamb," Hathach said quietly.

Esther frowned as she got up, walked around the room, and snatched her crown from the chair, throwing it to the floor.

Hathach's eyes followed her movements.

"This would never have happened if . . . Why did he adopt me if not to care for me like a parent? What kind of cousin is this?" Esther sobbed.

Hathach simply reached out to Esther and held her in his arms, receiving the full volume of her unspent grief.

The two sat shoulder to shoulder on the settee. Esther hung her head and waited for the criticism that never came. Finally, she whispered, "Do you think I'm ungrateful and selfish, Hathach?"

"My God, no, Esther," Hathach said, turning her shoulders to face him. "Your grief is your pain hidden behind your anger at Mordecai. You were young and alone, and the one who was supposed to love you, protect you like a parent . . ."

"Then I'm not so foolish? Of course it will be easier with me on the inside of the palace as Mordecai's power base, but I feel so dispensable. I felt so guilty about my resentment toward Mordecai, I even stopped praying for a while. I figured out his plot, but I just couldn't feel the fury and fear, only guilt. But you give me hope, Hathach."

"I'm so mad! I'm angry for both of us," Hathach stomped the floor with his foot and glowered. "People with power to mutilate young lives . . . enough suffering for a lifetime."

Esther took his wrist. "Mordecai is a threat to the king, and he is a brother Jew." She stood up resolute and faced Hathach. "I want to put all this aside now. Rage won't make us truly powerful, Hathach. There could be a way to do something powerful together, though. We have to think . . . and pray."

○

As it turned out, Esther never had her banquet as queen. Hathach and Esther had not seen each other for two days when word spread through the palace that the king had issued a new edict: All Jews in the land were to be destroyed. By royal decree. Somehow, on his own, Haman had found out about the plot to kill the king, had informed Ahasueras, and persuaded him that it was the Jews, led by Mordecai, who were responsible.

When Esther heard about the new edict, she dressed quickly in royal attire, donned her crown, and summoned Hathach, who was already on his way to her chambers. As he ran in, he was startled by Esther's appearance. "You really do look like a queen," he stammered. She looked so regal and so stern he bowed before her . . . twice.

"Hathach," she commanded, "stand up. It's time to act.

We are both Jews. Our people are in grave danger. What good is our secret, our safety, if our people die? Are you going to be Jewish or not, Hathach? No matter. I have decided to go before the king."

"No, no, you can't do that!" Hathach grabbed her hand. "It's certain death! Remember the rule: to go before the king without his summons means death! Besides, he might not even listen to you before you are dragged from the throne room. Esther, I will not let you do this thing."

"I am dressed. I am ready, Hathach." she said.

He stood tall in front of her. "I suppose, if you're really determined to do this, we could pray that the king extends to you the golden scepter. It's our only hope. But, Esther, it's still a terrible risk to defy royal protocol. Remember Vashti?"

"You told me the king has a golden scepter that he can give to the one who enjoys his favor. Whoever gets the scepter can make five petitions, and the king will grant them," she said. "But since I've not been summoned . . . "

Hathach replied, "Esther, the king can offer the scepter even to the one who breaks the summons rule."

She stared up at him. "What? Why didn't you tell me that before? My God, this means I have a chance."

Hathach nodded. "But you shouldn't risk your life, Esther, even for our people. Let me instead try to persuade Haman. Your life is worth too much."

"And yours, too," she said. "Hathach, you could be hanged for daring to petition a court official like Haman. I love you, and we share in a larger love, the love of Jews for Jews. You said 'our people' this time. I'm willing to take the risk for all of us. If I perish, I will perish." She turned to enter her inner chamber, looking once more toward Hathach. "Pray for me, Hathach. Pray."

O

Hathach didn't move.

She was gone. Gone. He fell into a morose silence. Groping his way back to his room, he sank to the floor. "Oh my God, what good am I? 'Pray,' she tells me. Pray. A useless Jew. What are the prayers of a eunuch, an exile, a Jew without a covenant worth? And what if she dies for this?" he sobbed. "Oh God, if you are there, if you hear me now, Esther is in danger and I am powerless. Save her. Please save her. Let the scepter be given her. Hear my prayer, thou God of my people, thou God of my people, thou God of my own heart."

Hathach repeated the ancient Mizpah blessing over and over again that night. *May the Lord watch between you and me when we are absent one from another . . . God is witness between you and me.*[2]

O

Esther stood silently in the king's garden that surrounded the court. The smell of fruit trees and acacia kept her senses alert. She had easily eluded the sleepy guard's attention. Now she could hardly breathe. 'Will the king notice me? Will he even come this way? Oh God, let me save my people. Let me just do this. If I perish, I will have at least done this,' she prayed.

Finally, her anxious waiting paid off. As she saw the king approaching her, she prepared herself for his question: "What are you doing here, my queen? I have not summoned you."

Esther held her head up. 'He doesn't sound angry,' she

[2]   This ancient *Mizpah* blessing, found in Genesis 31:49, 50b, is a prayer that God will oversee any agreement or covenant between two parties and guarantee that both will live up to it.

thought. 'He even looks a little kind.' Gathering her courage, Esther spoke up. "I could not wait for your summons, my Lord. Such is my audacious desire, oh King." She lowered her head, but not before she bathed his eager face in the radiance of her smile.

The king almost stammered. "But, you are not supposed . . ."

Esther, steeled by a sudden rush of energy, felt bold. She began to play the king's desire with the precision of a master violinist. 'This seduction is for salvation,' she murmured to herself. 'Oh God, let it work.'

The king reached beneath his robe and withdrew the golden scepter. He looked at her shyly. "I was watching you at a distance. I saw you enter. You are beautiful, more beautiful than any other woman. Here is my favor." The king held the scepter raised before him.

Esther reached out but could not touch the tip of the scepter, as was required by custom. She felt sudden fear. Was the king teasing her? She looked into his eyes. 'This is not the look of a torturer,' she thought.

The king waited.

The image of Hathach drifted into her imagination. Taking a deep breath, she rose on her toes and reached, this time extending her arm. There it was: the renowned golden tip. She touched it, put her whole hand over the golden orb, and felt its warmth.

○

"Hathach. If you are lurking there, show yourself. I am alive."

Hathach rushed forward and held out his arms to her, and hugged her. The two friends wept together.

"Tell. Tell me all about it," he said.

"Well, you remember the formula for requests of royalty? You taught it to me. After the king asks me my petition and guarantees that it will be granted, *even to the half of my kingdom*, then I say, '*If it pleases the king . . .*' "

Esther paused. She put her finger on his lips. "I made petition thus: '*If it pleases the king, let the king and Haman come tonight to a banquet that I have prepared for the king.*' "

"A banquet? A *banquet*!" Hathach drew back.

"Yes," she said. "Esther's banquet for the king and his evil vizier. *I* will give a banquet, not him."

"I'm sure the king loved that petition. Esther, what in God's name are you doing? A *banquet*? Do you think you can just charm these two men?"

"Yes . . . in God's name. I know what I'm doing. The banquet will be where I prepare the king to give even more than half his kingdom. And I will have not one, but two banquets. You know, Hathach, he seems to have longings. Not as repulsive as I thought . . ." She smiled slightly and stroked her chin. "But that doesn't matter. We need to save the Jews."

"Longings? Oh, Esther," Hathach sighed.

She smiled and hugged him. "The Lord has truly watched between us, as the ancient blessing says."

At Esther's request, Hathach inconspicuously attended the first banquet, watching impatiently, worried the whole time that Esther's plan would backfire.

The drama went on for hours. Eventually Hathach relaxed and marveled at Esther's sense of purpose and her poise as she entertained and flattered her guests. The king was delirious with pleasure. Haman, too, became quite drunk with wine and Esther's attentions.

"The noble Haman will have some more royal wine. It is delicious, isn't it? And you are such an asset to the king and his service," Esther spoke softly as she stroked his cheek and filled his glass.

"And King Ahasueras, my husband, my ruler. Ah." Esther slid her small body between Haman and Ahasueras. She faced the king, bent over to brush her lips across his forehead, then down his cheek toward his lips, stopping just short of his mouth. Then, turning his face toward her own, she moved her mouth slowly to his ear where she whispered her petition: "*If it pleases the king . . .*"

Haman came out of his stupor and realized what was happening. He rose and tottered toward the king, "My Lord majesty, you should re . . . uh . . . re . . . consider, consider. This may not be in your best interests . . ."

But it was too late. The king had assented to Esther's petition with a royal nod and the words, "It shall be granted you."

Then Esther surprised them all. She wanted just one petition granted—that the king alone be her guest at a second banquet.

O

"Esther, you were masterful, but I'm worried. What can you possibly want from a second banquet?" Hathach confronted her the next day.

"Trust me, my friend," was all that Esther would say.

'What will she do?' Hathach thought. 'Oh God, don't let her jeopardize herself. She is acting so familiar with the king.'

O

At the second banquet, Esther played the king with skill and subtle grace, almost as if she felt something beyond her mission. The next morning, she was eager to tell Hathach all she had accomplished.

"You know, Hathach, last night I even began to experience the king as a human being. He showed a remarkable degree of sensitivity even as he granted my difficult petitions. *You*, on the other hand . . . Hathach, what did you think you were *doing*? When you stepped out from behind the table, I thought surely the king would have you dismissed for interrupting! How could you take a risk like that? You scared me. Not only could I have lost you, but the whole plan might have been ruined! Thank God, Ahasueras didn't seem to notice!"

"It's not me I'm concerned about, Esther. It's you. I think you have gone beyond self-defense." Hathach responded, his eyes searching her intently.

"You scare me when you look like that, Hathach. Come, sit with me."

Hathach didn't move. "Esther, you've not only gotten the king to withdraw the edict against Jews by persuading him that this annihilation would be an insult to his reign, but you've also convinced him that falsely accusing the Jews was Haman's idea. And to top it off, the king has granted your request that Haman and all his sons hang on the very gallows Haman had constructed for Mordecai's hanging! But, Esther, this is not like you. Do you realize that you might have just unleashed a reign of terror, of wholesale violence? Is this divine justice?"

"Hathach, you must understand. It is the divine purpose. Jews have enemies. I had to do all in my power to ensure that the people of Israel would not be destroyed. The Jews must endure. It's not enough just to get rid of Haman and his family. I had to ask Ahasueras to allow the Jews to defend their honor, to be able to kill in self-defense."

"How will they know who the enemies are? How can anyone know?" Hathach folded his arms across his chest.

Esther was silent. She made one step toward Hathach, then stopped. She paced the room slowly, around and around, with a pensive look on her face.

Finally Esther spoke. "Hathach," she said, standing in front of him. "Hathach."

He looked at her.

"Hathach, are you still my friend?"

Hathach took a long time to answer. The two friends stood together, close enough to hear each other's breathing and see the tensions on each other's faces.

Hathach finally nodded and said, "Yes, Esther. I am your friend. I am your friend forever."

Esther smiled and reached for his hands. "And I am yours forever."

○

That entire sleepless night, Esther wept and prayed, her emotions ascending and descending like a scale of music. She knew that her friendship with Hathach was a gift from God. It had restored him to his faith and had given her the strength to fulfill her mission. She now felt the fullness of her power as a woman and as a Jew. 'So why is this next task so hard for me?' she wondered.

Esther knew what she had to do.

"I will ask the king for one more thing. God, you were my blessing when I risked my life for our people. Be a blessing to me now as I make this sacrifice. Though I will hate to lose his company, I will secure Hathach's freedom with a final petition."

A fresh flood of tears soaked the bed where she lay. "Can I bear it? Oh God, I don't know if I can. My first real friend. But I must. Should I tell Hathach? Have one more sweet moment with him, say goodbye? No, that would end in an argument. I will petition for Hathach's freedom, and he will leave. My dear, dear friend."

O

"*If it pleases the king,*" Esther began her final petition . . .

Leaving the throne room, Esther felt a fresh wave of sadness along with an extravagant satisfaction. The king had granted her request. Her friend would be free.

As she made her way back through the great hall, she stopped, suddenly arrested by the sight of one pillar. She had passed it many times before, but this time it stood out. It was where she had first seen Hathach. She put her hand against the pillar, remembering the mysterious fascination that had sprung up unbidden between them.

Leaning forward, Esther left a kiss and some tears on the cold marble column.

Considerations for Prayer and Reflection

". . . I will go to the king, though it is against the law;
and if I perish, I perish."

Esther 4:16b

For personal prayer:

Following the general guidelines for prayer described on page 16, reflect first on what the God Between might be doing between you and this midrash text:

- What got your attention?
- What brought a reaction, either positive or negative?
- Where did you feel the *hum* of the story in you?
- What relationship is the God-in-you calling you to explore through the story's characters or events?

For reflection:

"What's a nice girl like you doing in a place like this?" asked the Cheshire Cat of Alice in Wonderland. The cat might have asked the same thing of Esther as she trespassed in the king's garden, carried on an elicit friendship with a palace eunuch, hosted a banquet for potential enemies. (Except the wise cat would have known to say "a nice Jewish girl like you.")

What might have moved these two people, Esther and Hathach, caught together in a situation of powerlessness and oppression, to such courageous acts? I think their friendship is precisely what empowered them both to make sacrifices, take risks, endure loss.

If a woman like Esther came to me seeking Spiritual Direction or Pastoral Counseling about a decision to risk her life to save her best friend—and to lose her friend in the process—I might be tempted to dissuade her.

I might remind her of the current wisdom of the day about taking care of herself, not giving up everything for someone else, keeping the balance between self and other. I might question her motives and ask her to consider the consequences.

And of course, I would suggest that she bring her friend in for a session!

But then I might hear the conviction in her voice and intuit the honesty of her spiritual struggle. Then I would see the painful blend of love and loss in the tears in her eyes. Tears might spring to my own eyes. The God Between Us would draw my heart into relationship with her as I listened to her story from within the relational space we shared, and I would abandon much of the conventional wisdom of the day.

We would probably talk about her motives, and I might try to help her discern if her proposed self-sacrificial act were holy, rooted in the extravagant, unselfconscious love of God. I would ask her to describe her friend, their relationship and its meaning, and how she perceived the divine call moving her toward this action. And then we would do some grief work together, naming some of her losses, their impact on her life, and what ways she would have to take care of herself in the face of such loss.

The word "sacrifice" at its Latin root (*sacra* + *facere*) means "to make holy." For the Esthers and the Hathachs ancient and modern, the courage to act in love at the risk of one's life—and without clear answers and outcomes—is born out of the strength of a mutually growth-fostering relationship, be it personal or communal.

For further consideration on your own or in a group:

- What spiritual transformation do you see in Esther's and Hathach's friendship as a result of their sacrificial love?

- What healing connections do you see the God Between facilitating in Esther and Hathach's relationship?

- How do these connections empower them as individuals? How are these connections life-saving for each of them?

- How have you experienced the saving nature of friendship?

- What spiritual resources have you discovered in friendships?

- Have you ever made a holy sacrifice, or has a friend ever sacrificed for you?

- For what or whom would you sacrifice your life today?

A MOTHER'S CRY

MARY AND JESUS

(Mark 15:33-16:15)

O

*How does a mother resolve her feelings of abandonment
and let go of her child?*

O

"*Amma, Amma,* why have you forsaken me?" she heard
him accuse her.

Days, weeks, months after the execution of her son,
Mary's mind, as well as her soul and body, lived the horror of
helplessness. Watching Jesus suffer and die an agonizing death
had been torture, but that haunting vision had grown less vivid.
It was his parting words that held her captive.

She had heard them as she stood on the hillside, unable
to wrench her gaze from the unfolding agony before her: her son
nailed to a wooden cross, his life emptying out, painful breath
by painful breath. Dust from the milling crowd prickled her skin
and burned her eyes and nostrils. She felt the writhing restless-
ness of his dying agony as keenly as she had felt his life throes
kicking inside her belly some thirty years earlier.

The others had felt it, but not like Mary. They hadn't
heard his words, only a cry that had caused them to cringe, helpless as dry leaves before a strong wind. Joanna had covered her

eyes. Mary of Magdala had sunk to the ground and curled up like a fetus dropped out before its time. The mother of James had run away down the hill, stumbling and falling as she went. But Mary the mother of Jesus had stood straight. She smelled the stench of dried blood and the pungent odor of the vinegar that ran down his chest from the drink offering that had been put to his lips. She watched the slow rising of each breath drawn across his ribs. She heard the cackles and jeers of the crowd, the moans of the crucified, the echo of banging hammers still ringing in her ears, the wails of the women who, with Mary, had stayed close enough to be with Jesus to the end . . . and the words, the words that, to her, were the death sentence of her relationship with her son.

He was her son, the beloved. She had adored him even before she had seen him. She had birthed him in unimaginable pain, her life spared only because of Joseph's assistance. His hands thrust into her womb had the accuracy of love, fearless and undeterred. 'Oh, Joseph,' she had thought at Jesus' death, 'how I wish you were here to hold me in this far worse pain.'

From the beginning Mary's love for Jesus had been tinged with fear. She remembered Simeon's hard prophecy in the temple where they had taken the infant Jesus to be presented. The priest had prophesied great and terrible things for Jesus and told her that a sword would pierce her soul also (Luke 2:35). That prophecy hung inside her and plumbed her heart.

Mary had not always trusted Jesus' judgment. When he had shared his deepest thoughts and feelings with her, she received them without comment, keeping her distrust to herself. She wondered if she had been too cautious with him. At times she had sensed him holding back, too. Just before he had set out for Jerusalem, he had thrown his head onto her lap and cried out with fear, fear of Jerusalem, fear of Samaria, fear of the needs of his followers, fear of his own limitations, fear of the Holy One God he called *Abba*. She had stroked his neck and wept with him. Had he wanted more? Had he wanted her to tell him Jerusalem wasn't necessary?

At one time she had thought it would be better to stop being a mother, but most of the time she was confused and frightened for her son, frightened by the relentless force that drove him on what seemed to her a tragic course. They didn't talk about that. A mixture of sadness and longing, gentle and wordless, too vulnerable to touch, hovered between them like a butterfly that, if touched, would die.

'Oh, how I wanted to grasp him and hold him and protect him, even fight him!' she thought. 'But I was afraid. Of what? There was something unreachable in him. Something . . . I don't know. But if I had . . .'

O

Even today, Mary struggled against Jesus' final words accusing her of abandonment. Her friends told her that *wasn't* what he had said. They said he had been crying out the pain of his abandonment to *Abba*, his heavenly father, not Mary his mother. But Mary knew it had been hard to hear clearly out there on the dry, dusty, wind-blown hill.

"His last words are proof enough for me. You didn't hear him clearly. You said so yourself. I did," Mary declared to her friend.

"Mary," Mary Magdalene said soothingly, "you were a good mother! You taught Jesus everything. Why can't you see that? You're trapped in this crazy obsession, and it's killing you.

Most of your friends have abandoned you because you insist that you abandoned Jesus."

Mary shrugged.

"You were his mentor and spiritual guide, and you gave him your faith," Magdalene went on. "He confided in you. You did not forsake him. If anything, for God's sake, he forsook you!"

Mary looked up. "What? What do you mean?"

"Oh, forget it. I don't know what I mean, really," said Mary Magdalene. "He didn't leave you, exactly. He was always leaving. I just hate to see you suffer with guilt, Mary. It's not right. You're turning into a bitter old woman. I want to sympathize, but I don't . . . I don't think you've got it right."

"And this is why you hang on after all the others have left me, so you can convince me I'm wrong? I know how I feel," Mary retorted.

Mary Magdalene got up from her seat and began to pace. "I'm afraid I'm hurting you more, my dear friend," she said, pausing in front of Mary. "I loved Jesus, too. Sometimes my own grief leaves me senseless. But he loved you. Oh God, how he loved you. You don't understand. He used to talk about you and tell us about the things you taught him. He regretted not being able to come see you more, even felt torn. He told us the prayers you taught him, how when he was only three he would recite the Shemah morning and night, even showing off about it. And he told us how once he had broken one of his cousin's playthings, and you went with him for the apology. He wept for the memory that he didn't have to do it alone.

"And Jerusalem? My God, how he wrestled with that. He prayed and talked and prayed. He was scared, not really sure. He asked us if we thought he should just go home, be with you and take care of you as you aged. Mary, I think that was his heart's desire and devotion." Mary Magdalene took her eyes off Mary, who was staring at her.

She lowered her head and continued. "We persuaded him that the Jerusalem campaign was essential to his credibility and the mission. Maybe we should have . . ."

Mary nodded and looked away.

"Mary, look at me. Your son, your son Jesus, he . . . well . . . he . . . " Her voice drifted off. "I remember the times you spoke to me of your confusion and your hurt. You even once thought he rejected your love! Remember? You asked me if I thought he was possessed, crazy, like people were saying."

"Yes," Mary snapped. "And do you remember your reply? You said, 'In a way, yes.' That's what you said!"

"But you knew what I meant. Possessed by the divine spirit. That's . . ."

"Different? Good, I suppose?"

"Well . . ."

"Mary of Magdala," Mary said. "I know you loved him, too, love of a different kind. But didn't you ever feel like I do: guilty because you didn't do enough and angry because you couldn't do more?"

"Yes, but . . . "

"Hush, woman, no need to defend my relationship with my son; no need to defend yours either," Mary declared. "I know you mean well, but I heard his words of accusation, and you don't know what that means to a mother's heart. He didn't forsake me. It was I who did the abandoning. Do you hear me?"

After a long hesitation Mary Magdalene responded, "We all are grieving now. There are so many questions about what to do, how to do it. We have had a vision of angels . . . "

"*You* had a vision of angels?" Mary interrupted.

"Well, yes, and, and reassurance of resurrection, and, and . . ."

A morose silence fell over the two women. Mary Magdalene left after a short time.

'A vision of angels. Hmph. What a foolish girl,' Mary thought after her friend left. 'Thinking Jesus had forsaken me! But I know the truth. I heard his words from the cross. *I* was the one who forsook him. I didn't mean to, God knows, but I could have stopped him, especially when he was so young and following after John the Baptizer. Now John . . . there's a boy who broke his mother's heart. Oh God, Elizabeth's grief. But she at least didn't let her son go without protest. I can remember her incessant tirades, weepings, and naggings. That boy was so stubborn! But what did she think she could do? Stop him? Save him? From what? Whatever it was, she failed, and John died a hideous death, too, like my Jesus. Oh, my Jesus.'

Mary held back tears. 'And me? Why didn't I nag Jesus more? He was less irascible than John. He might have heeded my word. Why was I so passive? Who did I think he was, anyway? He was just my son, only my beloved son. Maybe he was crazy after all, and I failed him. If only Elizabeth were here to talk to.'

○

Mary got up from her chair and began to busy herself with housework. She worked steadily until dusk, exhausting herself. It was the only way she could get any sleep. She lived now in a little house in Ephesus. The others kept in touch with her some, especially John his disciple, but they were making plans, trying to figure out how to carry on the mission without Jesus, trying to remember just what the mission was. They talked, sometimes excitedly, of resurrection and peace and spiritual empowerment, but Mary couldn't see much evidence of that yet. Of course, it had been only nine months. She didn't have much hope, really. Her boy had been a dreamer, faithful and beautiful—a beautiful dreamer.

"I knew all about his dreams, most of them, I suppose. How could I have felt so left out? What did I expect?" she muttered. "But how can so few followers carry out such a mission?"

Opening her cupboard, she lifted out two small vials of oil. She had saved them for a special occasion or need, maybe even a mother's blessing of a son before marriage. Mary stroked one vessel with her forefinger. 'These are of no use now. Silly to save,' she thought, gently replacing the oils on the shelf and closing the cupboard door.

'I wonder why I don't pray much any more,' Mary pondered. 'Guilt? Fear? Shame? Or have I lost trust? I thought it was the right thing to do, encouraging him even though I knew the peril. So I didn't stop him. But did I let it go too far? He was so passive in the end, they said. Like me. Why didn't he defend himself? I should have defended him myself. Oh God,' she laughed. 'I, a woman? No credibility at all. But I could have coached the men, and they could have . . . I shouldn't have entrusted so much of all this to you, God. I think I could have . . . Oh my God, I wish I could pray again!'

O

As the days passed by into one year, then two, then three, Mary's dry bitterness of soul surrounded her like a thick wall. The others came to visit less and less, and even Mary Magdalene didn't see her often now. "It would take God alone to break through this one," Mary Magdalene had said. Mary thought it was just as well. Jesus was dead, and that was that. Perhaps even God was dead. Only the bleak remembrance of Jesus' last words remained: *Amma*.

'What would it take to relieve me?' Mary wondered. 'God alone, as Mary Magdalene said? Not much hope for that, I'm sure. Maybe an appearance? If my son would visit me as he has the others . . . If Mary Magdalene can have such an experience, why can't I? I am the mother after all. The *mother*! I bore him. I loved him. Joseph and I did the hard work. And we taught Jesus Torah. It was right to do that, wasn't it? And I carried on after Joseph died. But what has a vision of Jesus gotten his close followers anyway? They still flounder around, talking it up, but . . . Ah, I keep thinking all this over and over. I'm sick of myself.'

O

For three years, Mary endured her suffering. Three years of self-recrimination and self-reduction. Three years of godlessness and fighting against despair. She wore these burdens as a mantle about her slumping shoulders. She detested the heaviness, but the hope that the pain might somehow atone for her inability to save her son gave her some satisfaction. At times she felt threatened by a darkness so profound she thought it might actually be the pit of Sheol, the netherworld of death. Housework was all that kept her mobile, but it provided no real satisfaction.

Every evening Mary lit one candle, a small remembrance of her son and the One he had called *Abba*. She wondered why she did even that small gesture.

"I'm ready to die. I'm old now, and my life has no meaning," she said aloud one night, staring at the tiny, fluttering flame. She thought of the stars lazily adrift in the night sky and longed to be absorbed into their serenity. A sigh, unexpected and unbidden, surged through her tired frame and passed out into the universe as a whispered prayer: "My soul, my soul, come forth, come forth . . . I am not helped . . . not blessed . . . My God, my God, why have you forsaken me?"

That night, Mary dreamed of her son Jesus. She saw him as an infant, drowsily content at her bare nipple like a round fuzzy peach, ripe and ready to drop from its branch. She saw him as a little boy playing with his father's tools and inventing little sayings as he chattered to no one in particular. She saw him as a teen, demanding more affection and silent understanding than she could muster, and at the same time closing her out of his private world. She saw him robust and at the height of his young maleness. She saw his tears and his look of longing the last time they were together, just before he headed for Jerusalem. It was as if he wanted to take her along. She would have gone. Yes, she would have gone with him, right then. But they could not communicate such desires, could not cling to each other as mother and son.

Then she saw him dead, breathless and without motion, nailed to a cruel wooden cross. She saw him, too, in a new form, not quite recognizable, but beautiful. It looked as if he were smiling at her, beckoning her to come. In the dream Mary felt uncertain. What did this new Jesus hold? Would he stay still long enough to be consoled, to console? Or would he disappear, forsake her again? Was he still her son?

As the dream faded, Mary slipped into the passage of her dying. A ferocious peace snatched the armor from her soul and

enfolded her bare truth into its strength. Her last words just before her last breath were, "Oh, it's you, son."

And God-in-Mary said, "*Yes*," as she dropped into her final sleep.

O

Three days later, when Mary Magdalene and John arrived to try one more time to convince their friend of her faithfulness as a mother, they found her stiffened body. They laid
her gently on a mat on the floor and began to anoint her with oils
they found stashed in the cupboard, oils once used for blessing
and healing, oils long forgotten, now remembered.

Considerations for Prayer and Reflection

"Listen. To live is to be marked.
To live is to change, to acquire the words of a story,
and that is the only celebration we mortals really know.
In perfect stillness, frankly, I've only found sorrow."

Barbara Kingsolver, THE POISONWOOD BIBLE

For personal prayer:

Following the guidelines for prayer described on page 16, reflect first on what the God Between might be doing between you and this midrash text:

- What got your attention?
- What brought a reaction, either positive or negative?
- Where did you feel the *hum* of the story in you?
- What relationship is the God-in-you calling you to explore through the story's characters or events?

For reflection:

When I found out that my oldest son had decided to marry, I wept. Not because I didn't like the woman he loved, nor because it was an ill-considered decision. I wept because of a sudden, deep sense of loss. The way of things, it has seemed to me, is that boys and adult sons grow more and more distant from their mothers or get "adopted" by a wife's family. While mothers and daughters fight, mothers and sons separate.

Jesus' mother would be no exception to this, I thought. Yet the biblical accounts of Mary's relationship with Jesus are spotty and incomplete. We can only intuit with our own feelings the heart's pull between them. After the nativity, Mary's is a presence that periodically invades the flow of the story without much integration. How sad.

In light of the remarkable devotion to Mary that grew up and still prevails in the Christian church, I have wondered why, at the climax of the great tradition's story, there is no account of a post-resurrection appearance of Jesus to his mother. Was she forgotten by God or simply slighted, as so many other women were, by the gospel writers? Has the truth of Mary's sorrow been ignored or whitewashed by the image of her obediential faith that the culture of the church wishes to maintain as a model for women? Do mothers of sons deny the truth of their own love-filled sorrow?

C. S. Lewis tells us that, as a boy when his mother died, he closed off his heart to love and chose safety. Later, as a man, he chose suffering in order to have love. The minute the human heart opens to love, it immediately opens to the grief of its loss as well.

Michelangelo's "Pieta," a sculptural midrash of Mary holding her dead son, is a perfect expression of love and grief. As such, it could belong to every mother/son relationship that is characterized by longing, love, and loss. The capacity to love and suffer with dignity is itself a source of hope and beauty for us all. Thank you, Mary.

For further consideration on your own or in a group:

- How do you see the God Between working to heal the abandonment feelings that shaped Mary's perception of her relationship to her son?

- In what ways have you experienced the sorrow of love?

- Have you, like Mary, ever been troubled by a feeling that you imagined belonged to someone else . . . but was really your own?

- For you, what are the hardest things about letting go?

- What spiritual transformations have you experienced in relationships, or in yourself, when you have let go?

A DIFFERENT KIND OF LOVE

DAVID AND JONATHAN

(I Samuel 13:16-II Samuel 1:1)

O

How is the love between two men a blessing?

O

Jonathan sat alone in the large dining hall, resting his head on the long table and wondering if his father would come to dine tonight. Storm clouds flitted by, catching his eye as he turned to lay his head on one arm.

'Is that music I hear?' Jonathan wondered. 'No, it can't be. All I ever hear these days is my father's anger. Saul, king and mighty warrior covered with armor, all the time battling, all the time angry. We used to be close. He's probably still mad about the honey. How was I to know that he had made an oath to the Lord God, swearing a fast for all of us until all the enemy was avenged? All I wanted to do was reward my troops with a bit of something sweet. Who would have thought eating honey would cause such a big ruckus? My God, he tried to kill me over it. Thank God, the people interceded and the smell of more victories assuaged him.'

Jonathan stood up and pointed his finger toward the other end of the table where Saul usually sat. "Oh, great Saul, what are you? Remember your son. As the Lord God, Yahweh, lives, I too have fought and won mightily for my people. An amazing victory we won over the Philistines, just me and my trusty armor bearer, Micah, tricking them into thinking there were more of us, and then just the two of us alone killed many. Ah, you were so proud of me that day."

Jonathan stared at the empty chair, imagining his father's dark eyes flashing, as tears shot into his own eyes. He banged the table and fell to his knees. " You foolish man! Doing everything just right, building altars, making vows and keeping all the rituals. Oh God, is this what you want? And are you displeased with me, too? I didn't know that I broke the fast, the king's oath. But oh, the honey brightened my eyes and delighted my tongue. So I ate. Teach me your ways, Lord, teach me."

Gentle strains of music slowly penetrated the sound of his breathing and the murmurs of his prayer. The music threaded him like a needle and drew him up and forth to follow. It came from his father's quarters. 'Saul doesn't play like this,' Jonathan thought. 'In fact, Saul doesn't play at all! What *is* this?' Jonathan rose to follow the sound. Slowing his step and steadying his breath, he came to Saul's door and, finding it ajar, he peered in.

Saul sat slumped in a chair. He barely lifted his head at the intrusion, then let it fall back against his chest.

'Is he entranced? Should I try to wake him? He doesn't look angry . . .'

The lyre's pitch suddenly soared, stretching the little instrument's capacity. And then Jonathan saw David. He nearly lost his balance and fell into the room. 'Who is this?' he wondered. 'I must meet this young musician.'

O

"My father is indeed calm tonight," Jonathan said, watching his father at the other end of the dining table. "I couldn't help but notice . . . "

"Yes," Saul nearly smiled. "You heard David play, then."

"David? He is called David?" Jonathan moved to the edge of his seat.

"David the shepherd boy, son of Jesse." Saul fixed Jonathan in his gaze. "Ah, my son, you would fall into the boy's lure. My Jonathan, you would fall."

"No, I . . ."

"Oh, you would, my son," Saul sneered. "But David is mine. His music croons to my sour soul and causes my acid heart to melt. It is like the fragrant breath of God to me. I cherish the lad and his music. He is mine."

"May I meet this David?" Jonathan asked.

"He will be my armor bearer," Saul said.

"Armor bearer?" Jonathan's voice dropped.

"Yes. He will be my loyal and heroic comrade. Nothing will come between us as we make conquests in the Lord's name. I am the king of Israel, and David will be my music, my soul, my armor." Saul yawned and rose from the table without another word.

'Soon I will meet this David, my father's armor bearer. And then we'll see . . . ' thought Jonathan.

When David came to take his official place as the king's servant, Jonathan ran from their house ahead of Saul to meet him. Jonathan stood before David. Together the two looked like saplings, straight and supple. Their eyes met, and it seemed to Jonathan that his inhale met David's exhale. 'We are breathing as one,' he thought, excitement rising in his chest.

"Who are you?" David asked, smiling.

"I am Jonathan, the king's son," Jonathan answered.

'This is a beautiful man,' David thought, his eyes widening.

Jonathan stripped off his cloak and draped it over David's shoulders, gripping their round smoothness for just a moment, and David responded by lifting his shoulders to place them into the security of Jonathan's cupped hands.

"Well, I see you have arrived safely," Saul announced, coming up behind Jonathan and pushing him aside with a firm movement of his right hand. David could only nod as he watched Saul holding out a set of armor. "This is my armor, sword, and lap belt. These are assurances of victories to come. You will carry them in my honor. They are symbols of our covenant: You will be loyal and serve me in battle, and I will protect you and keep you in my household." Saul laid the armor at David's feet.

David stood in silence until he noticed Jonathan urgently motioning to him to pick up the armor. David then reached for the treasure, bowing to Saul.

Saul smiled broadly and turned toward Jonathan, beckoning him to stand at this side. "This is my son, Jonathan. His fealty is beyond reproach." With that pronouncement, Saul smacked Jonathan on the back hard enough to cause him to lurch forward. Jonathan knew that, beneath those seemingly praise-filled words, Saul was thinking of his oath and the honey.

After Saul left, David and Jonathan stared at each other. David wondered what had just happened but said nothing until Jonathan spoke. "Don't mind my father. He has odd moods, and he's obsessed with the rules for everything. Here, you can put the armor down now."

David carefully placed the armor on the ground beside him and stood to face Jonathan again. He put his hand to his head.

"My brother, do you feel overwhelmed?" Jonathan asked. "My father has a way of making people feel unsteady. Here, sit down on this plank."

'It isn't your father,' David thought as he sat down.

"David," Jonathan continued, sitting beside him. "David. What a noble name. You will be a fine warrior, a tribute to the royal conquests."

David edged away from Jonathan, at the same time sitting erect and smiling. "Yes," he said, "I believe I will be a great warrior. I've longed for a chance to prove myself as a real soldier. You've probably heard how I slew the giant Goliath of Gath with only a slingshot. How much more I will do with real equipment!"

"No need to boast. I'm sure you are valiant. David?" Jonathan asked suddenly. "Would you eat if you were hungry?"

"What a question. Of course!" David answered. "Wouldn't you?"

"Yes, but . . ."

"What's on your mind, Jonathan? Ah, you are hungry. Is that it? You're hungry." David tugged at Jonathan's arm and punched him lightly as he began to laugh.

"Don't tease," Jonathan said, at the same time thinking, 'I want to tell him about the honey, and I want to tell him how I feel.' Jonathan pulled David toward him and raised him to his feet. "Stand here, my brother. I will give you something else."

"You have given me your cloak," said David, wrapping the garment around his torso. "It's warm."

Jonathan drew David's hands apart, releasing their grasp

on the cloak, which dropped to the ground. David bent to pick up the cloak again, but Jonathan shook his head, raised his right hand in a gesture to wait, and turned to walk back toward the house.

Soon he returned, carrying another set of armor. "More armor, my brother. More armor for you. Don't look so shocked. This is a different kind of gift." With that, Jonathan proceeded to clothe David in the armor, slowly and with care, placing the breastplate on his chest, fastening the lap belt around his waist, and securing the sword in its scabbard. Before Jonathan stepped back to admire his handiwork, he rested his hand on the breastplate and looked intently at David's face.

David lowered his head under Jonathan's steady gaze. He yanked at the belt Jonathan had fastened around his waist and looked up to see Jonathan watching his movements with measured care. David pulled the belt even tighter, catching his breath with each tug.

"You have Saul's armor for battle, and now you have mine," Jonathan said, smiling at David. "Have I upset you?"

David scowled at Jonathan. "I'm just wondering why you're giving me your own armor. Is it a symbol of future victories for us?"

Jonathan didn't answer, only smiled and walked away.

'What is he doing to me?' thought David. 'I am a warrior. Why do I need more armor, let alone armor bestowed by the son of Saul? I need none of these things.' David began to strut around, brandishing the sword and slashing the air, delighting in the wind-slicing whisper of the sharp blade. "I am a man. I am a man of God."

As he strode around, David remembered his days as a shepherd boy in the hills. 'Days on end, I just sat watching the boring sheep graze. Oh, how I wanted to be a hero, tall and brave and strong. There was no one to talk to, so I talked to Yahweh, the God of my people. "Make me a hero, God," I'd pray. Make me strong, stronger than all the pillars of heaven itself, strong like a rock, a rock that never fails." That was my prayer, and now it's come true.'

David sat down on the plank and, piece by piece, removed the armor Jonathan had given him. He laid it down, sat on the ground, and let his hands fall empty to his lap, wishing for his shepherd's staff. "Oh God, I feel so empty. Why am I here? I don't feel strong at all. Make me strong. Who is this Jonathan, who makes my legs feel as if they will crumble under me? How could he and his armor be the answer to my prayer? Is he? Oh God, make me strong. Make me strong."

David wept.

○

As the years progressed, David did become strong. He excelled in the service of Saul's army and outstripped his rank as armor bearer. The people sang songs to David; the women danced and played tambourines; all the people laughed and chanted: "Saul has killed his thousands and David his tens of thousands" (I Samuel 18:7).

○

"David has moved his allegiance from lyre to armor, from music to war, my father," Jonathan complained. "This war-raging is exhilarating but tiresome, don't you think? I could use more music."

"David is preoccupied with his military gains. Fool," Saul growled. "He knows nothing. I am king, and the people will pay allegiance to me alone. Do you hear me, my son? *Do* you?" Saul shouted at Jonathan, unsheathing his sword as he spoke. "I will have this boy killed. Killed. Do you hear?"

Jonathan nodded and backed away. Outside, he walked and prayed for David. "Oh God, my love for him is great. I fear for his life. My father is fierce and irrational. Oh, David, you are the darling of the people, but you are a fool to threaten Saul's power and prestige. The armor I gave you will not protect you from the king's wrath, but it is all my love. God, you are in this love. Or is this just my idea? Does David know of your presence in our friendship? Are you the God of honey or of war, as my father says?"

As Jonathan walked, his pace increased, and prayer flowed from his lips like the forbidden honey that had once so delighted him, dribbling and oozing in thick, golden curls from the edges of his mouth and down into his beard.

"God's love is pure honey, sweet and thick and flowing plenteously. Do you hear me? Hear me, God?" Jonathan fell to his knees.

Returning to his father's house, Jonathan followed the music. He found David in his quarters, hunched over the lyre, his fingers nimbly plying and plucking.

"Music like honey, my friend," Jonathan said. "I'm glad we are here alone."

David put the lyre down. "I need a friend in this house. Come and embrace me, Jonathan."

"My armor is a sign of my friendship, David," Jonathan said. "Do you think our friendship is of God?"

"Oh, I suppose. It doesn't matter much to me," David said.

"What matters?" Jonathan said.

"Well, you matter. From the moment I saw you, I knew you were beautiful . . ." David said.

"That's only my looks, David," Jonathan interrupted.

"Only looks?" David laughed.

'Ah, Lord God of the universe,' David thought, 'he thinks I mean appearance. But I do. Didn't God give us looks and faces so that we might see souls?' Laughing softly, David gave his friend's shoulder a gentle shove, and they laughed together.

"I will play you some music now, my friend."

As David played, the music wrapped the two friends in its embrace. By the time David had put his lyre down, Jonathan had decided to tell him about the honey and Saul's rage.

"Do you think God was offended?"

David was silent for a moment, then spoke. "I think you have God confused with Saul. How do you know the will of God was not with the people who urged that you be spared? They saved your life."

"Well . . ."

"Jonathan, God is not your father, and your father is not God." David put his hand on Jonathan's shoulder. "You're trembling. Come and sit by me."

"David, I love you," Jonathan said. "What do you think God thinks of this?"

"I don't know." David shrugged.

"Aren't there rules for the friendship we share?" Jonathan sat back a bit and looked at David.

"Well, a covenant has rules. We have a covenant in the armor, I guess. Isn't that enough?" David asked. "You worry too much about rules. That's tedious."

Standing up, David grabbed Jonathan's hands and pulled him toward him. "This is different. See? Can you feel my heart beating against yours? Can you catch the scent of my breath on your face? Feel the brush of my beard in yours? This is *different*, Jonathan." David pulled Jonathan closer, then thrust him away. Tears showed in Jonathan's eyes.

"Have I hurt you?" David asked.

"No," Jonathan said and left the room.

David picked up his lyre and resumed playing. The music filled him with grief, each note piercing his heart. "He is in me in a way I have never felt," David said aloud. "He makes time and space open up. He makes me feel safe. Why do I treat him roughly? I don't owe devotion to him as I do my father or to Saul. That's part of the difference. We don't owe each other anything, so neither of us can control the course of our love by playing on indebtedness. We have a different kind of love. Jonathan would say all covenants have rules. But he is not sure of the rules. Does your love have rules, God?" David shouted out through the open window. "Does it?"

"*No, but yours does,*" said God-in-David, the voice of his soul.

David left the room, walking swiftly down the corridor toward the great hall.

"David . . . "

"Who's calling me?" he said, turning around quickly. David saw Michal, Saul's daughter, silhouetted in the shadows of the doorway to her room. He approached her, thinking, 'She is lovely. She could help my career and perhaps keep Saul and his predatory ways at bay.'

"Michal, I'm glad to see you," he said. She smiled and held out her hand, drawing David to her. As they kissed, David felt the press of Michal against him. 'Yes, I will have her,' he thought.

◯

A few days later, David found Jonathan in the garden where they had first met, where David had received the gift of Jonathan's armor.

"Jonathan, I plan to marry your sister, Michal," David told his friend. "It is a good thing for the royal family and for me. It is right and good. And I love her."

"You mean *she* loves you," Jonathan muttered and walked away, for he knew of his sister's longings.

"Jonathan, wait. Don't just walk away. Are you upset?" David tried to detain his friend, but Jonathan pulled away and left.

David's hands dropped to his sides. "Some friend," he pouted. "I thought he might be pleased. Are you pleased, God? Saul fairly begged me to be his son-in-law. I imagine he thinks this will tame me. And it's a marriage of love and political benefit. Oh, Jonathan, are you jealous? I am faithful, but the love of a woman is right and necessary. You of all people should know that this covenant has rules in accord with the holy plan."

David headed toward the woods, Jonathan's favorite place, in search of his friend. "Jonathan. Jonathan. Are you out there?"

Jonathan heard David's voice and stood against a tree, waiting.

Finally spotting him, David approached on the run, calling. "I looked for you? Are you mad at me? I knew I could find you with the trees. Why are you so distressed? Marriage is . . . marriage . . ."

"Marriage is marriage. Covenant is covenant. Friendship is friendship. And love is love."

"Yes," David said.

"*I* love," Jonathan folded his arms across his chest and smiled weakly at David.

"Oh, for God's sake, Jonathan. Talk plainly. Your words are here and there, there and here. They are like grit in the eye. I can't see what you mean."

"Dear, dear David," Jonathan said, pushing his friend. How do you think I feel? You dangle your love before me, and now you are marrying my *sister*? What do you mean by this, little covenant brother? Speak!"

David sat down against the tree. Jonathan uncrossed his arms and sat next to his friend, their shoulders touching, muscles tight with tension. They both stared straight ahead, saying nothing.

Finally, Jonathan broke the silence. "What are the rules of love, David? Our kind of love. What are the rules?"

"Oh, shut up, Jonathan. Just shut up. You're always trying to keep everything safe."

"That's true, David, but you are so free, you don't know where you're going."

"Well, I'm going ahead with my life, that's where," David said, his gaze shooting outward, away from Jonathan. "I'm making alliances, securing my position. I will be king one day, king of Israel." David's back straightened against the tree.

"Yes? And whose path are you following to get there?" Jonathan asked. "David, you underestimate Saul's wrath. He only wants you in the family because . . ."

"I guessed all that, Jonathan," David said. "You asked whose path? I follow the God of Israel, of course. The path of the Lord."

"So far it's a pretty crooked path, David."

The two men faced each other, and suddenly they were both laughing and hugging and slapping the tree. "That's it," David shouted. "I'm making the path . . . making it myself, crooked and all. Thank you, Jonathan. Thank you. You make me see crooked things straight. Only the eye of God knows the true course of my destiny."

"In the meantime, keep walking, is that it?" Jonathan chuckled. "Ah, David."

As their laughter subsided, David rolled onto his back, his head falling into Jonathan's lap. Jonathan took hold of David's head with his hands, making a gentle cradle. David lay very still so as not to disturb the gentle grip of his friend's hands. Jonathan bent over and kissed David, softly, like the flutter of butterfly wings.

"These must be the rules," David mumbled as he fell asleep.

O

"My father is enraged, David. He believes you are out to usurp his power," exclaimed Michal. "He even thinks the people want you to be king instead of him. He plots to kill you and has instructed his men to stab you in your sleep at night. But I have a plan. I will place an idol in your bed, covered with your clothes and a web of goat's hair. That will buy you some time, but you must go immediately!"

David held Michal in his arms and whispered his thanks. "I will be back, and I will be back triumphant. Tell your brother, Jonathan."

Michal nodded. "Jonathan helped me with this plan,

David. Hide in one of the caves in the hills until Jonathan lets you know that it's safe to return. Many people are devoted to you. You will be able to gather a following."

David knew Michal couldn't say it, but he would defeat her father and unseat him one day. He left that night, taking enough food for several days.

O

"Loyal you are not, daughter!" Saul raged at Michal. "How dare you deceive your own father and the king of Israel?"

"David would have killed me, my father. I was afraid," Michal said, lowering her head.

Saul turned his back to her, concealing a smirk. 'Ah, maybe my daughter is still loyal to me after all,' he thought. 'What could she do? A husband who would take her life to spare his own. Such evil must be scoured from the land, my land. David is no respecter of men and an abuser of women. I am right to want him dead. I am a defender of the faith, a hero for my God, a good father, and a righteous man." Saul's face collapsed in defeat around his tear-filled eyes, even as he held himself erect leaving Michal's house.

O

David made his way to Naioth in Ramah where he found temporary sanctuary with Samuel the prophet as he roamed the hills. He languished and pined, praying aloud, "I am alone again in the hills. I know I'm not strong. Oh God, send me Jonathan."

Eventually Jonathan learned from Samuel of David's hiding place and went to his friend. Jonathan peered into the darkness of the cave where David crouched. The two men locked eyes as they listened to the sounds of each other's breathing. Neither moved

"David, there is more at stake than the dangers of war and political power," Jonathan finally said.

"My life, for one thing," David replied.

Jonathan stooped and entered the cave. Taking his friend's hand, he said, "More than danger unites us."

"I don't like being a refugee on the run. Fleeing, hiding in caves, scrounging for food. Forced to live like an animal with only a step between me and death." David scratched the ground with a stick. "You say more than danger unites us. I say we are both in danger. Your father knows you favor me. He may begin to hide his plans from you. He may even decide to kill you, too. What do you mean, more than danger unites us?"

Jonathan silently looked at David.

'Oh God,' David thought. 'Jonathan looks sad now. What did I do to upset him? It's hard to love without rules. I get it and then I don't.' The musty air pressed in on David, and he brooded in Jonathan's silence. 'I have to get out of here. I can't stand it.' David pushed Jonathan aside and ran out.

Jonathan followed. "You have a valiant and earnest spirit, David, even though you may feel terrified."

"You're laughing at me. God is laughing at me," David shouted. "What good is a valiant spirit to a prisoner?"

Jonathan did not interrupt his friend.

"God, you mock me," David went on. "Show me your face. I'm sick of mystery. Jonathan knows the rules for everything. I know the rules of war. I know the rules of politics. I know the rules of filial piety and marriage. What are the rules for someone running for his life?"

Jonathan knelt beside David and held him as he sobbed. "God's rules are like honey, David, sweet and nourishing, not like the rules we know. I will make us a fire to warm us."

Soon David and Jonathan were warming their hands before a small flame. David relaxed. "Well, Jonathan," he said softly, "tell me about Saul's plans."

Jonathan grinned broadly. "You'll never believe it. He thinks you are gone and he is safe. What a limited mind he has!"

The two men sat on their haunches before the fire, David stoking it lightly with the end of a stick.

"Tell Michal of my gratitude and my love. I love her, too, you know. I'm tangled up inside with too much love. I'm not good at it. Do you understand?"

Jonathan nodded. "David, David, it's your political ambitions."

"What do you mean?" David looked intently at his friend's face as light and shadow flickered over it.

"I'm not sure," Jonathan said. "I mean, for you, is God in our love or in your idea of kingship?"

David said nothing.

"All I know is that I love you as I love my own life," continued Jonathan.

"You are risking your life for me," David said. "Your father would kill you if he knew you were here. This isn't just honey!"

"Yes, but I know how to be faithful to my father, too, and I know his ways. Michal and I will be all right, and you will be protected."

"Oh God, Michal. I have betrayed her love and yours . . . and Saul's and . . . How can you keep all these loyalties straight in your heart all at once? I can only do one passion at a time."

"Yes, that's it. You live by one rule: impetuous, exclusive passion. You're not selfish because your passion opens you up to more. But you are single-hearted."

David cried. "Oh, Jonathan, I do love you. Do you know I do?"

Jonathan nodded slowly, more than once. David reached one hand to touch his friend's face. With the other he wiped at the flow of tears that drenched his own face. Eventually the two fell asleep, warmed by the fire's embers.

◯

At dawn David awoke first. "Jonathan, wake up. We need a plan." He shook his friend awake.

"All right, all right. God, you are like an arrow in flight." Jonathan had already thought through the details. Step by step, he described an elaborate plan by which he would let David know Saul's every move.

"Jonathan, you've done it," said David, with relief. "Maybe I really will survive, even build up my forces, gain power. Your strategies will save me. You will see. And then . . ."

"And then?"

"Oh, then. Well, we will be together again." David strutted around, feeling his usual self-confidence returning to him. "Yes. I will wear your armor in battle, and it will make me mighty."

"Do not wear my armor in a battle, David. It means something else between us, not war."

"Oh, you and your silly ideas. Well, all right. I will keep the armor as a symbol of our relationship, our covenant of love. And we will be together soon, without worries or fears."

'He doesn't understand,' Jonathan thought as he shook his head. 'But he will soon enough. Thank God he knows the love of God. That love will hold him fast.'

"Well, what is wrong with you now? Why do you shake your head as if you disagree with me?" David took hold of Jonathan's shirt. " Of course we will be together soon."

"It will be safer if I stay with my father and help him win his battles," Jonathan said slowly. "This is what he really wants. It will make him feel confident, and you will be able to execute your own plans without much interference."

David nodded. "I see," he said. "Jonathan, you have given me back my strength. I will make everything work out to benefit both of us. As God is my witness, I swear it." Even as he spoke, he thought, 'He doesn't understand. I will be able to make this happen the way I want it. As God is my witness, I swear it.'

Jonathan started to turn, but David reached for his arm. He set Jonathan's shoulders straight with his grip. They stood together motionless, taking in and holding on to each other's souls. David broke away first, stepping back from Jonathan and bowing. David stayed deeply bowed until Jonathan finally turned and walked away.

Then David fell forward and lay on the ground, repeating aloud the ancient blessing as he wept: *"The Lord watch between you and me while we are absent one from another."* [3]

○

---

[3] This ancient *Mizpah* blessing, found in Genesis 31:49, is a prayer that God will oversee any agreement or covenant between two parties and guarantee that both will live up to it.

Word of Jonathan's death came to David at the battle-front, ten years later.

"How can you be sure? Are you sure *both* Saul and his son Jonathan are dead?" David grabbed the messenger's shirt and shook him. "Who are you, anyway?"

The young man stammered, his face ashen, "I am . . . I'm . . . I was an armor bearer."

"An armor bearer? Whose armor did you carry? Answer me!" David was frantic. "Whose armor?" he screeched.

David's men gathered around to watch the fury of their great leader gone mad. The boy fell into a faint. David fell face down beside him. One man reached toward the boy and dragged him away from David. The others helped, but no one approached David.

"What did you see?" one of the men asked the boy as he revived.

The boy looked toward David. "I was in the region of Mount Gilboa where a battle had taken place. The men of Israel had fled, fearing further loss. All of them were running in different directions, spilling out over the mountain. Many, including Saul's sons, were slain by the Philistine armies. Saul begged me to thrust his sword through him, but I was too frightened to kill the Lord's anointed." The boy paused, looking in horror at David. "Look! He's eating the dirt of the ground. Oh God, what will become of us?"

"Continue your story, boy. David will recover. He always does."

The boy shrugged and went on. "Well, Saul then took his own sword and fell on it. That's what he did. He actually set it in the ground and threw his full weight onto the blade. He howled. It was grotesque. Blood spewed out all over, and Saul writhed in pain and prayed for mercy. I shut my eyes. Should I have been loyal to my master? Should I have killed him as he wanted? I always obeyed him, but . . . I just ran away. I got word later that his three sons had died, too." The boy's voice faded away.

"Loyalty can kill you," said one of the men nearby. "David bears little loyalty to his family, his wife, or anyone, really. It is said he was loyal to Jonathan, but I wonder."

"No, that's not true. David twice spared King Saul's life, didn't he?" asked the armor bearer. "He was merciful to a king who wanted to kill him. Isn't that loyalty?"

"More like love, I'd say," said a different man in the group. "More like love, son."

"Do you think David *loved* Saul? Saul, his enemy? That even I can't believe." The boy frowned. "David who killed his ten thousands to Saul's meager thousands . . . not that David."

"Yes, that passionate, enigmatic lover of souls. That David who one day could kill wantonly, and then the next day feed us with the bread of the Presence. Said he learned that from Jonathan . . . something about honey."

The boy listened attentively as the man continued. "David doesn't follow a lot of rules or codes of honors. He really has just one rule: 'to love the Lord God with all his heart and with all his mind and with all his body.' And sometimes that one rule makes him do some pretty strange things."

Just then David sighed in anguish and began to weep. The men stood silent, helplessly watching the great warrior's grief.

○

David arose and intoned his lamentation in a loud, almost angry voice. "How the mighty have fallen, have fallen, have fallen. Ah, Saul and your son Jonathan, your son Jonathan, Jonathan your son, your son."

David stood silhouetted against the darkening sky, praising and cursing the God he loved. "My God, this is more than I can bear. Jonathan lies slain. Why didn't you kill me instead?" he screamed. "I thought our covenant was sacred. Didn't that mean you would protect us? I thought one day Jonathan and I would . . . Tell me your ways, you silent, cruel potentate, you holy king."

David sobbed and raged. Then he waited for God to answer.

The velvet silence said nothing. Nothing soothed the crushing sorrow, a pain more intense than battle wounds, pain that crushed David's soul, pain that only a word from the divine mouth itself could comfort, pain that only the divine countenance could bear to hold in its gaze, pain that only God's most delicate messenger could touch and heal.

David at last fell asleep, the name of Jonathan kissing at his lips like the flutter of butterfly wings.

Considerations for Prayer and Reflection

". . . greatly beloved were you to me; your love to me
was wonderful, passing the love of women."

II Samuel 1:26

For personal prayer:

Following the guidelines for prayer described on page 16, reflect first on what the God Between might be doing between you and this midrash text:

- What got your attention?
- What brought a reaction, either positive or negative?
- Where did you feel the *hum* of the story in you?
- What relationship is the God-in-you calling you to explore through the story's characters or events?

For reflection:

David's poignant lament after he heard of the death of Jonathan signals a depth of love between the two men, dropped unexpectedly upon the vast canvass of military exploits and political power dynamics that characterized the young Israel's struggles to forge its destiny as a nation among nations, with David as its king. The passion shared between the two men springs up from time to time throughout the saga like a rose, out of place, yet remarkable in its delicate beauty and strength.

As I noticed and became attracted to this "rose," I wondered what it meant and why it was even noted in the first place. Why was Jonathan, the only one of Saul's sons who is given name and place in the history, there at all? Was he only a literary device to assure David's rise to power over Saul? And what did David mean that his love for Jonathan surpassed his love for women—which in David's life had been considerable?

Today, the rules, definitions, and categories of socially acceptable love have greatly expanded. There is much confusion in the minds of faithful people. Many, myself included, wrestle with sincere hearts and minds to sort out and understand different gender categories and sexual behaviors. And here in the middle of it all, in the ancient text of the Hebrew scriptures, is this passionate love between two men, one a king of Israel and a beloved hero of the faith. What is the God Between trying to tell us?

After reading commentary and analyzing to exhaustion, I collapsed into acceptance. Ellen Gilchrist in her novel *Sarah Conley* comments that sometimes life is so complex, it cannot be answered by anything but acceptance. David and Jonathan were praying, faithful men. Were they homosexuals? Bisexuals?

Sometimes our mental efforts to categorize, and therefore contain, love kills it. Sometimes love slashes through all the boundaries and bursts the confines of what we expect or can predict. What seems precious to me, and a blessing, is that the love between David and Jonathan needs no category. They loved in the context of faith, and the love of God was in them.

When love partakes of the divine, it forgoes human constraints and transcends human constructs. It breaks the rules—like a rose on a battlefield or a butterfly in a man's kiss.

For further consideration on your own or in a group:

- How do you see blessing wrought by the God Between in the midrash story of David's and Jonathan's relationship?

- Do you think God blesses rule-breakers who have spiritual integrity like David's?

- Have you ever chosen safety over the desires of your heart and body?

- Have you experienced a love that has felt right spiritually and been wrong according to expectations, rules, or categories of acceptability in church, society or family? How was God with you in this experience?

The Garden Restored

ADAM AND EVE

Genesis 2:4b-3

How can a marriage survive a very deep wound?

ONE DAY:[4] FEAR

A young married couple, Adam and Eve, live in Eden, a beautiful garden. It is where they met and where they have begun their new life together. Beautiful and lush, the garden has everything in abundance, and the couple lacks for nothing. There is only one fruit tree from which they are not allowed to pick and eat. All other food and comforts are theirs for the taking. They believe their marriage is made in heaven. Everything is perfect, and all their needs are met. They have no fear. There is, in fact, a touch of the eternal in their lives.

Then suddenly everything changes.

---

[4] I have called the first section of this story One Day, to use a concept of time from the creation story. In it there is no chronological ordering of creation: The water appears in Genesis 1:2 with no account of its creation. The point is that the *first* day is simply one day, evening and morning with no reference to the idea of "firstness." In creation, the business of that one day is nothing more or less than the radical transformation of reality from the oneness of God to more. (For more on this interpretive framework see Avivah Zornberg, *Genesis: The Beginning of Desire,* The Jewish Publication Society, 1995.) Thus, Adam and Eve's one day is not first in chronology or importance but simply the day of a mysterious new order of reality and pattern of relations. This day encompasses all the others.

○

"Oh my God, Adam, look!" Eve shouted, tugging at Adam's shoulders. "Turn around . . . "

Together they stared at the place they had called home, now transformed into a frightening spectacle: huge, winged cherubim, one green and one brown, their flashing black eyes menacing, guarded the entrance to their garden. Adam and Eve could see flames, tongues of fire lapping and leaping from above the walls.

"It will all burn down," Adam shrieked, rushing toward the entrance to Eden. "Our beautiful home is in flames! Oh God, what can we do?"

Eve grabbed Adam's arm, yelling, "No, Adam. Don't go in there, you'll be killed. It's too late, too late." She sobbed as she fell to her knees, dragging Adam down with her, and covered her face with her hands, shaking uncontrollably.

Adam crouched beside her on the dirt, holding onto Eve for dear life, unable to steady either her hysteria or his own sudden, overwhelming feeling of helplessness. He felt like a rag. 'There's nothing I can do,' he thought, burying his face in Eve's shoulder, wetting it with his tears.

Eve let one hand drop from her face to look again at the flaming horror. "Adam, look," she said, pulling at his hair to raise his head. "I can just see the tips of the trees' golden foliage over the top of the wall. Maybe only the wall is burning, and we could . . . "

"Return home?" Adam looked at her hopeful face, smudged with tears and reflecting the fiery glow even from a distance. He broke into sobs that racked his body as he fell back away from Eve and lay on the ground face down, pounding with his fists "No. There's no hope."

"But . . ."

"No . . ."

Eve watched Adam's distress and went numb. 'How will we survive?' she wondered, looking around at the bleak landscape. She ran her hands through the hard, gritty soil on which she sat. "I'm afraid to live out here," she said aloud and moved closer to Adam. "I'm so scared. I don't know where God is."

Adam sat up and put his arms around her. "Neither do I."

Nestled in each other's grasp, they rocked back and forth like a cradle that has lost its baby. Adam kneaded the flesh of her arm. Eve nuzzled his hand. "Will we ever see home again? The place where we met, first kissed, made love on green velvet mosses? Where we knew YHWH, God? [5] Oh Adam, can we even talk to God? Will God answer? Where is God now? Maybe the garden will be restored."

Adam was silent, stroking her hair and thinking to himself how soft it was and how he hadn't noticed that before.

"Adam, I'm cold. I can hardly breathe. How will we eat? Where will we sleep? Oh God, do you think this all happened because we ate that forbidden fruit?"

'She has so many questions,' Adam thought. 'How *will* we survive? How would I know?'

"Adam," Eve continued. "Do you think YHWH, God will relent? YHWH, God is good. Maybe God will take us back. Maybe this is just a big display of power to scare us."

"It's working," Adam said glumly.

'I'm pretty scared, too,' he thought. 'Can't she see we're

[5]   *YHWH, God* is the name for God used by Everett Fox in his translation, *The Five Books of Moses* (NY: Schocken Books, 1996).

out of Eden for good? This isn't a game . . . it's serious."

The couple stayed silent for a time, still watching the spectacle of their lost home. Eve stood and moved a distance from Adam. They were, for the first time, separate, alone in their fears.

Eve kicked at some loose stones. She looked at Adam. 'Who is this man, my beloved?' she wondered. 'There he sits in his gloomy silence. It was never this bad before. Will he talk to me?'

"Adam, there are no trees outside of Eden. Look around. We have no shelter, no food, no trees for wisdom or food, for shade or sweet scent. No plants at all. No animals for company and extra love."

Adam closed his eyes and turned away from Eve. 'Who is this, my beloved? I've never heard her complain like this.'

"We need to move," Adam said aloud. "The sun will set soon, and we need a place to sleep."

"And what happens after the sun sets?" Eve asked. "Will it rise again soon?"

"How should I know!" he retorted. "All I know is it won't be the same as in Eden." He got up and began to walk farther away from Eden. "Are you coming?" he scowled.

Eve was still craning her neck toward Eden, looking for some shred of hope. Adam moved forward and, after a longing last look, Eve followed, thinking to herself, 'God, I hate fruit!'

The couple turned their backs on their former home and walked eastward, shrunken inkblots bled onto the pages of an unwritten history.

ONE NIGHT: MEMORY

While Adam stayed alert, restless, watchful, Eve slept in the blissful oblivion of sheer exhaustion. God-in-Eve reaped her memory and tilled the soil of her knowledge until it bore good fruit.

O

"Look, Adam, look at that fruit. Isn't it beautiful?" asked Eve. "Oh, I can just reach it if I stand on tiptoe. See?"

Adam did see, noticing as well the grace of her naked form reaching and swaying. "I see," he said aloud.

Eve went on, "This tree's the one we should leave alone, right? Isn't that what you understood? It had something to do with knowing. Remember? But we agreed. This tree was more attractive, its fruit more enticing, than all the others."

Adam did remember. The tree had always bothered him. It stood majestic in the garden, never out of view. He didn't understand why it was forbidden, and he didn't want to think YHWH, God was capricious. Adam thought he could decide whether or not to eat its fruit. He had the freedom of the gods . . . which also annoyed him.

"Aren't you afraid, Eve?" Adam asked. "This tree might not be good for us. We have plenty of fruit already."

"Oh, I know," Eve replied. "But that's not the point, really. I mean, how much is too much isn't my question. Oh, don't look so sober!" She jumped up to give the hanging fruit a pat and, heavy with ripeness, it broke from the branch and plummeted to the ground. Gasping, Eve stepped back as if the innocent piece of fruit might suddenly attack them.

But Adam darted quickly to the fruit, his eyes wide with amazement. "Eve, look. It's ours. Wait, don't back away. Can't you see? It's off the tree and fallen. You barely touched it, and it came to us."

Suddenly the tall grass rustled near Eve's feet. Although she was

not normally afraid of snakes—or any other creatures in the gar-
den—Eve was startled She leapt aside, tripped, and fell forward.
Putting her hands out to catch her fall, she landed with them wrapped
around the sun-rippled fruit. The huge orb lay in her grasp, a perfect fit.
She kissed it, and it tasted so sweet she felt her whole body explode. "Yes,"
she whispered. "Yes."

Adam fell upon Eve, moving his hands from her shoulders slowly
down her arms until his hands encircled hers. They clasped the fruit to-
gether for what seemed like a very long time. They lay, feeling the down of
skin against skin, hearing the thump of their hearts. Together they said,
"Yes."

THE SECOND DAY: ANGER

When Eve woke up on the morning of the second day away from home, she looked immediately toward the east. The sun was there. She sighed, rubbed her sore arm muscles, and sat up.

"*You are not alone,*" said God-in-Eve.

"What?" said Eve aloud, looking around. This voice sounded like YHWH, God, but she heard it as if it came from within herself. It was so faint, she wondered if she had really heard it. She batted it away with her hand as if it were a gnat and called to Adam.

"Let's go," she said.

"Where to?" he asked.

"Somewhere. Food. Come on."

The couple began walking They trudged on with more and more difficulty. The rocks and pebbles seemed to multiply as they kept walking side by side. They didn't know how to stop, and they didn't know how to keep going.

"Oh, my feet miss grass, soft, green grass," Eve moaned, stopping to look back at the now-distant garden, a dark hole surrounded by a fiery glow. "We've been trudging along for hours. I'm tired."

"Tired already?" Adam snarled. "Who knows how long we'll be walking like this. Obviously YHWH, God is punishing us and wants us to die."

"Oh, for God's sake." Eve put her hands on her hips and made a face at Adam. "Well, I have a choice, and I'm stopping to rest. At least YHWH, God gave us skins for clothing. Did you notice?" Eve asked. "And we're not dead. You noticed that, too, of course. Besides, it's not my fault."

Adam glared at her and sat down. They stopped and rested.

Eve sat on the ground and peeled away the top of her garment slightly to peek at herself. She glimpsed the tilt of her breast rising above the swell of her belly. She shuddered and yanked the garment back, glancing at Adam to see if he had noticed her failed vanity. "Don't look at me," she hissed.

"What?" asked Adam.

"Nothing. I was just talking to God, not you."

"Hmph. Where will that get you?" said Adam, who refused to sit down.

'What does he know, God,' she thought frowning. 'I didn't used to be embarrassed at the sight of myself. I am beautiful in thy sight, am I not? But what does that matter now. We have to find some food. God, you were always the provider of good fruit. Where will we find fruit now? If it weren't for fruit, we'd be happy ever after. But right now, I'd give my life for a piece, just one piece of luscious fruit. Oh God.'

Adam tried to talk to God. He had never had to pray before . . . he had never *had* to try. "Where are you?" he called out, looking quickly at Eve to see if she had heard him.

She hadn't. She was looking back toward Eden again. 'I curse you, Eden. I curse you, God. I curse you, Adam,' Eve snarled to herself between clenched teeth. 'Adam should have stopped us from eating that fruit. He is the sensible one. Now he blames me for the whole thing, I know.'

Eve turned and shouted to Adam. "You blame me for this, don't you?"

Adam said nothing.

Eve groaned to herself, wiping her tears with the corner of her sleeve. "Sleeve. A sleeve. *My* sleeve." She kissed it and then held out her arm toward Adam. "We have clothes, soft skins. This means something, Adam. Something about God caring about us after all, not wanting us to perish naked out here, like you think. God has clothed us, and it is good." She flapped her garment open and closed, teasing him with glimpses of her nudity and prancing back and forth before him. She flushed as she twirled around.

"What are you trying to prove? We wouldn't need clothes if you . . ." Adam stopped short.

"Shut up, Adam. You stifle me."

"Enough. Let's go!" Adam said and began to walk away.

Clouds enveloped the landscape as twilight stole in. Adam got so far ahead, Eve couldn't see him. She called out, "Adam? Where are you? Wait!"

He didn't answer but stopped to watch as Eve picked her way through stones and shrubs up a hill toward him. 'She looks like some kind of night animal stumbling along. Stupid woman. Find your way back to me in the dark. Then see how much God loves you!'

Eve approached panting. "I can't go on. I'm exhausted."
"You're always *something*."

Eve turned her back on Adam, lay down, and curled up, her wriggling hips searching for a soft place in the ground. She tucked her coat snugly around her frame and pillowed her head with her hands.

Adam stared at Eve. He was fatigued beyond rest. He decided to make another attempt to talk to God. "How will I do this? I'm not adequate for this new life. I can't measure up to Eve's expectations. She's always ahead of me, even now in falling asleep. How can she sleep? "

As he watched Eve, he thought of the day they were together, eating fruit and loving the taste. It helped him settle into sleep, but not before he had planned his speech for the morning . . . if there were another morning. He would tell Eve that it was because of her impetuosity (which he once found charming) that their beautiful life was ruined. He would tell her that the rib story he had told her—how she had been perfectly formed from his own bone and flesh—was a lie. They weren't alike at all. They were strangers.

O

Eve awoke early, raising her stiff body to a kneeling position. Looking eastward, she saw a crisp sliver of sun. 'Thank God, another dawning. Something reliable in this miserable world.' She looked around at the barren landscape. 'Oh, I miss Eden's beautiful greens, oranges, purples, blues, yellows, whites. And I'm starved. I must find food.'

Eve did not wake Adam but made her way across the hilltop where they had slept. She spotted a small grove of trees at a distance. 'Trees. Are those *trees*?' Eve ran with excitement toward the grove. She grabbed one of the lower branches and tasted a leaf, curling her lip at its bitter taste. She foraged deeper into the grove and found grass and sand and berries, small red blessings, a whole bush full. She shoved them recklessly into her mouth and stashed as many as she could in her pocket. 'Fruit!'

Going a bit farther into the thicket, she came to a clearing and found water. 'Water. Thank God! Water.' Eve dropped to her knees, cupping her berry-reddened hands to scoop the water as fast as she could into her mouth. It wasn't fast enough, so she bent farther, touched her lips to the pool, and lapped the water, relishing its course into her body where its mercy relieved.

Then Eve began to cry. She thought of another fruit, another tree. 'Why wasn't Adam more cautious, more like himself, that day? He was more like me! And me, I was more like him. I'm not afraid of snakes. Why did I jump like that? I wonder . . . But how quickly everything else seemed unimportant as we fondled and ate the fruit, licking its succulent juices from each other's chins and lips. Oh yes.'

Eve left the grove and walked swiftly back to Adam. She woke him from a sound sleep. "Look, Adam, I've found water and food. Berries." She began to pelt him with the little red berries. He leapt up, flailing his arm. Eve teased him. "Silly. This is breakfast on the outside. More fruit. See?" She spit berries in his direction, taunting, laughing too loudly. "Eat," she laughed. "Eat."

Adam watched her stuff her mouth and smear the dye all over her face.

Then he took the fruit and ate.

THE THIRD DAY: SORROW

Eve and Adam traveled for many months over dry, barren terrain, looking for fruitful land on which to settle. They had decided that Eve's small grove was not big enough, and berries alone wouldn't do. They needed more fruit. They walked without talk, but each of them talked to YHWH, God. The desert of their relationship was as arid as the soil they trod. Their garden home was a distant memory. They needed rain. They needed seed.

YHWH, God was silent.

"We have to talk," Eve said one day. "Adam, we have to."

Adam was silent.

That night Eve dreamed. In her dream she stood alone on a hillside, looking out over vast expanses of water. The air was pungent with salt. She sucked in the air, pore by pore, and her flesh moistened. She turned to face the land, fearful it would be unfriendly. To her right she saw hordes of people, led by Adam, marching toward her. Adam looked strong, as he had in the garden. He advanced, followed by people of different sizes, colors, ages. It was a mighty throng. In the dream she felt puzzled. What did these people want? Where were they going? Then she looked to her left where she saw patches of green and purple and golden foliage, spread like carpet to a horizon of mountains. She looked back to her right and then again to the left and knew she had to choose: staying with Adam and his people or going on alone in hopes of finding her own paradise.

Eve awoke and prayed. "What would you have me do, YHWH, God? Is this a message? You're as silent as Adam! My heart will break with all this silence. God, make him talk. It's so lonely. There aren't even animals to love around here. We have only seen small ones, and animals in Eden didn't scurry off in such a frightened way. All the animals in Eden were friendly; even wolves were playmates. I don't know what to do. Oh God, I miss his touch so much."

In desperation, Eve shook Adam from sleep. "We're married, for God's sake. Married!"

"So?" Adam grunted.

"Married people are supposed to talk, communicate. I'm sick of living with your silence. What are you, depressed? All we have is each other. Married people are supposed to make love."

"Have sex, you mean?"

"Of course, idiot. What is wrong with you?" she shouted. Eve stood defiantly in front of him.

"There's nothing wrong with me, Eve. Nothing. It's your fault we're in this predicament to begin with. You're so smart. You with all the ideas. I don't want to talk to you. I don't even want to see your ugly, dirty face." He turned his back on her.

"I'll run away if you don't speak to me," she threatened.

"And just where would you go? You can't survive without me. You're dependent on me." Adam looked at her.

"And just what are you? *Not* dependent, I suppose." Eve turned away from him this time, tears streaking down her face.

Adam spit on the ground and walked away.

"Don't you just feel like crying?" she shouted at his back.

"I can't," he said flatly and kept walking.

'Neither can I,' she thought but said nothing. 'Ours is such a dry sorrow. Oh God, so dry. I've tried. I've tried with Adam. He doesn't want me. He doesn't love me. Oh God, what shall I do?'

She remembered her dream, with its choice. Was God

asking her what she wanted? 'Maybe the expanse of water in the dream is all our uncried tears.'

That day they didn't walk together, let alone talk. They stayed apart. Eve thought about her dream. 'In my dream I felt powerful. But it seemed I would get lost, submerged in Adam and his numbers. I'd rather be alone. Am I to be alone, God?'

The setting sun brought Eve and Adam back to their sleeping place where they lay silently. Another day gone.

Eve looked at Adam's sleeping form, the easy rise and fall of his breathing. She got up quietly, picked up the clothing YHWH, God had provided, as well as some other garments and a grass mat she had woven, and walked away.

"I choose alone."

With that, she left, carrying the crushing weight of her sorrow.

She didn't look back.

THE FOURTH DAY: SORROW

When Adam awoke, he at first didn't notice that Eve was gone. Accustomed to life within himself, he began his day alone. He was troubled by a dream he had had and sat for some time. In the dream Eve had walked off into the sea. He thought she was going to swim, but she just kept walking in and disappeared. He waited, watched for her to surface. She didn't. Finally, he went after her, feeling scared. He ran toward the water, but as he ran, the water receded. He ran faster, but the water that contained Eve moved away from him, and he could not reach her. His heart pounded as he thought about it.

Then he noticed Eve was gone.

'Probably just looking for food,' Adam thought. 'When

she returns, we'll eat and begin the day's trek. God, let us find a place to settle today. Just like I was in my dream, I am helpless. God, make me powerful.'

Adam waited for Eve, but she did not return.

"Oh God, my dream. Is this it? Has she left? Was my dream a prediction? Is this my fate? Answer me."

YHWH, God was silent.

"Eve, Eve, Eve," he called out.

Only silence met his call.

Adam walked out in different directions and distances from their site, circling like a nervous vulture. He rummaged through their things, again and again, searching in vain. Eve's belongings were gone. Her mat was gone.

Adam surveyed the landscape as he had so many times. Today it looked even more barren and hostile, even more dusty and fruitless. Tortured with self-loathing, Adam kept repeating to himself, "This is my fault. My fault." He curled into a ball, sorrow racking him from head to toe. Adam sobbed, "Oh my God, YHWH, God, where are you? Where? Take this pain away from me. I can't bear this much." He cried and groaned until he felt empty.

It was then that YHWH, God spoke his name: "*Adam.*"

Adam didn't move. He couldn't believe he heard the familiar voice, only it came from deep inside him—even though he looked frantically around to see where it was coming from.

"*Adam.*"

This time, Adam perked up. He listened, savoring the sound. "Is that . . . ? Is that you?" Adam stood up and looked around. "I know this voice. Oh God, is it you? Oh, please don't leave me alone. Talk to me. Where is Eve?" Adam's questions for God tumbled out one after another. "Speak more, speak more. Please answer," Adam begged.

God was silent.

'Only my name,' Adam thought. 'That's not enough. I want conversation. I want it like it used to be. I want advice, reassurance. What good is just hearing my name?'

As he sat there, hungry for God's voice, Adam began to repeat his own name, over and over. Soon quieter, gentler tears flowed. Adam rocked himself to sleep and rested for long hours in peace.

THE FIFTH DAY: FREEDOM

Eve had played a desperate wild card by running away from Adam. She knew it, but she felt wild and free, even though the risks of her situation surfaced in her mind now and then. To keep them at bay, she concentrated on her dream vision. And she prayed more than ever.

"YHWH, God, it's hard to talk to you this new way. Do we have a relationship still? I can't hear you the way I did in Eden, but I'll keep talking anyway and try to listen hard for your answer. I want to find a fertile place to settle, another paradise . . . sort of."

Eve moved at a swift pace over several days, eating whatever fruits and greens she could find. She even developed a taste for some roots she would never have considered tasting in Eden; now their sharp flavors awakened her palate. Her conversations with God continued, but there were changes. Eve made up a regular morning prayer: "I bless you and praise you for another day of life. Shine in me like the sun shines on me. And make me a blessing. Amen." She liked the prayer, and before long it became a comforter, a recipe for starting the day.

For evening Eve made up another prayer: "Holy One of blessing, your presence fills the universe. Your presence fills me." And as she prayed, she spread her arms and legs wide and breathed long breaths to feel God. Eve was getting the idea that God was inside her. "I am your home, God. What a delicious idea," Eve laughed. "I always thought you were outside us, sort of like a friendly watch dog. I hope you're not insulted, but that's the way it seemed to me in Eden. Eden . . . I didn't have to think there as much as I do now. Everything was just *done*. It was paradise really, but something was missing. How could that be? I'm finding so much new knowledge. Is that what that tree with the forbidden fruit was all about?"

Eve enjoyed her morning and evening prayer rituals. Like parentheses, they surrounded her day with faith and kept her moving, lifting her step and deepening her knowing of herself and everything around her. She even prayed for Adam. "I am lonely, and I miss Adam so much. God, how is he? Care for him too, please. But I'm not really all that lonely because I'm discovering a whole new place. It's hard . . . but it's interesting." Eve danced her next few steps. "I feel so free."

One day Eve decided to talk to God about her problems with Adam and about their relationship. It was a subject she had avoided because she had so many difficult questions. "Adam scared me, God. He just wouldn't budge. He got so far away from me. Was there something more I should have done? Adam blamed me for the fruit, but he ate with as much relish as I did. He even told me it was all right because we didn't pick it. It just fell. That was one of those little half-truths that gets you in trouble when you take them at face value. But even before it fell, I did want that fruit. I thought it would bring some excitement. You know, God, Eden was truly idyllic, but let's face it, it was a little boring. Like Adam could be when he was right and good all the time. That made me so mad."

YHWH, God smiled.

Eve sat down to rest. She stroked her leg with the palm of her hand. "My bones and muscles feel strong from so much work, so much stretching. That's it! That's what was missing in Eden. No stretch! Everything was too easy. Look at my body now, God. Oooh, so strong." She gave God a demonstration of this new wonder. "I will go on. Will I find my dream's paradise? Will Adam come? I will go on."

Near evening, a few days later, Eve noticed that the landscape and the air had changed. She had been climbing slowly up a slope for a few days, and the air suddenly felt moist against her cheeks. "A few more steps and I will be at the top of this rise. What's on the other side? More of the same? Oh God, not more desert. I will close my eyes and let my new muscles tell me when I have reached flat ground. Then I will open my eyes and hope to see my dream come true. Please, God."

The majesty of what she saw at the top of the hill stopped her breath. "It *is* my dream, or almost. It's unbelievable." Eve fell to her knees. "Oh my God, my God, thank you. This is good. This is very good."

Water, trees, and blooming flowers garnished the scene with blue and green and brown and yellow and deep rose. Eve ran down the hill. "I will live here. This will be my home. " She touched the flowers, kissed the grassy ground, hugged trees, grabbed fruit from branches low and high, and bathed naked in the water. Oh, this is where God is. And where I should be."

Shaking herself dry, Eve sprawled on the grass near the still waters. "Holy One of blessing, your presence fills the universe. Your presence fills me. Amen. And amen."

THE SIXTH DAY: LOVE

When Adam awoke, the sun was well into the sky. He let it soak into his skin as he thought of Eve. 'What has happened to me? I feel different. Everything in my life was lost, everything that mattered, that gave me reason to breathe: my beloved, my home, my sense of sanctuary and safety. But I feel all right. I even feel powerful. Why?' Adam remembered his name and how lovingly he had cradled it in his mind. Adam, the human one. *Adam.*

Glad for the clear blue sky and soft breezes, he began his trek. 'Eve is out there somewhere, and I will find her. She was right. I should have talked to her. I was too afraid and angry. I made myself hard as a rock, sure that being expelled from Eden was her fault and sure I wasn't good enough for her. Oh God, let me find her. Please.' He pictured Eve in his mind's eye, conjuring every inch of her body.

As he was making camp one evening, he heard a sound and jumped. Usually the wilderness was still at night. He listened. It was a growl. This time Adam saw the animal, crouched and snarling, exposing sharp fangs, ears flattened, eyes gleaming.

"Wolf," Adam called. "Wolf of my own naming. I know you, wolf. I named you, remember? Come. I could use your company."

The wolf growled again and put one leg forward. Adam suddenly sensed that this creature was not like the wolves in Eden. This wolf didn't know him. "There were no unfriendly beasts in Eden. This one looks fierce. This one is danger," Adam said to himself. He felt his heart skip to his throat.

"Oh wolf," he began. In mellow tones Adam began to talk to the wolf, and as he did, his fear subsided. "Oh wolf, listen to me. You are God's own creation and you are good. I, too, am God's creature and I am good. We are good, good together."

Adam talked softly, not moving or taking a step. The wolf continued to growl but made no move. Adam talked on into the night, never taking his eyes off the wolf's. Eventually, the wolf's growling softened. She let her front legs slide forward and her rump settle beneath her. Alert, eyes blinking, she stared at Adam as he talked. Very slowly Adam moved into a squat. Still talking to the wolf, he spread out his mat and, one careful movement after another, he lowered his body onto the mat until he was prone.

'I could be destroyed tonight,' he thought as he bid the wolf goodnight, closed his eyes, spaced his words, and before long stopped talking and slept.

In the morning Adam saw that the wolf was gone. 'Thank you, God. Thank you. I am alive.' He patted his body all over to make sure. 'How odd . . . I miss that wolf.' As he prepared to journey forth in search of Eve, Adam wondered if he were headed in the right direction. 'I've headed east. Why east? Eve would have headed east, following the dawning sun. If I find Eve . . . oh God, let me find her . . . I will tell her I'm sorry. I will ask for forgiveness. I will ask her to marry me . . . really marry me, all of me.'

With the passage of more and more days, Adam realized he might never find Eve. He might never be able to marry her for real, yet he proceeded with determination. Adam felt as if he walked in love, love he wanted to give to Eve. If only . . .

THE SEVENTH DAY: MARRIAGE

Expecting more barren landscape, Adam dragged himself to the top of a hill and looked down. Astonishing lush, blue-green beauty greeted him. He blinked. 'Surely *this* is paradise. My God, what a sight. You have prepared a feast in the wilderness. Oh, I want to bring Eve here.'

Adam didn't run down the hill but advanced slowly, gazing at the beautiful sight as if it might disappear if he looked aside.

Watching from behind a tree, Eve stared at the lone figure creeping down the hill. 'Isn't that like Adam to keep his pace cautious, deliberate . . . so beautifully, entirely Adam. It must be him.'

Eve loved the absolute sovereignty she had over her own life. It was intoxicating, but she knew that something was missing. The sight of Adam churned her heart and made her flesh leap, but she didn't run toward him. "Oh God, I'm straining forward and pulling back, split in two. Do I go forward or stay back? Oh, hold me together."

Adam's heart drummed as he caught sight of Eve. 'It's Eve!' he thought. 'She's here. Everything I've been hoping for. Make me enough, YHWH, God. Oh, make me enough to make our relationship thrive.'

"Adam?" Eve called out.

"Yes, it's me. Adam."

Eve smiled. "It's me, too. Eve."

"It's us," they said almost together. Laughing, they embraced and kissed and kissed, their bodies beginning the conversation.

In the days that followed, Adam and Eve shared their souls with relish as they talked and planted a garden from seeds and pods Eve had saved. They ran their fingers through the moist, rich soil. They told each other hard things and easy things, loving things and hating things, stunted things and whole things, blessings and curses, all the while marveling at how fertile the soil of their relationship had stayed.

"What's the hardest thing you have to tell me?" Eve asked him one day.

"It's what I've already told you in so many ways. I felt so much terror that I didn't know if I could go on without you. But I was also ashamed. I was so depressed, I couldn't move. You know how slowly I move anyway."

"And I laughed at you," she said. "Oh, Adam, I'm sorry."

"Your laughter made it worse," he admitted. "I loved your bright laugh and I hated it. I hated you for being so confident and me so inadequate. Now tell me, Eve, what's your hardest thing?"

"Isn't this planting hard enough? Okay, okay . . . I prayed without hearing YHWH, God's voice," she said, her hands on her hips. 'But I prayed anyway."

Adam nodded. "I did, too. And one day I heard the old YHWH, God call my name."

Eve gazed up at the sky. "Adam, I missed you. There were times when my whole body pulsed with the remembered rhythm of our love . . . but I loved my freedom, too. And there is something we need to talk about. Something still separates you from me."

Adam listened expectantly.

"I didn't . . . I thought . . ." Tears fell down her cheek. "I thought YHWH, God created you first and you were best. There. Now you know."

Adam gasped. "Eve, I can't believe it. Because of the rib

story? And all this time I've thought you were so confident, you were so sure of yourself in everything, even the fruit. That story bothered you so much?"

"Oh, I didn't believe that story. But . . . I did, a little."

"Sit up, beloved," Adam said. "I will tell you a story, a story YHWH, God told me long ago, a beautiful story."

Eve sat up, and Adam began. "In the beginning when YHWH, God decided to make us, we were created in God's own image, by divine purpose. We were created the same. In the divine image we are the same, of exactly the same value in God's eyes. And we are supposed to be that way in our own eyes. And that's the truth. Do you see? It's beautiful."

"Why didn't you tell me this story before, Adam?" Eve stood up.

"I'm sorry, Eve" he said, looking up. "I felt inferior. I wanted to bring you down a notch or two."

"And you told me a phony story to make me feel bad about myself?"

"Well, there's some truth to the idea that we are bone of bone and flesh of flesh, both human ones." Adam stood up, facing Eve.

"Don't make excuses, Adam. What you did was cruel," said Eve.

"Don't we have a forgiveness plant in this garden?" he asked. "And Eve, are you sure it was only the rib story that caused you to feel insecure?"

She was silent, then shook her head.

They stood facing each other for some time. Eve didn't know whether to lunge at him or run away again. Adam didn't know whether to build a fence and shut her out or kneel before her.

"So we're even then," Eve spoke at last. "We're even, Adam. You withheld the beautiful story from me, which made me doubt myself. And I withheld my secret insecurity from you, letting you think I was more confident and sure of myself than I really was."

"Well, well, well," Adam said. "So, are there any other weeds in our garden?"

The couple squared off. "Yours is dandelion," Eve said with a smirk.

"And yours is goldenrod," he shouted.

"Milkweed."

"Stinkweed."

"Crabgrass."

"Jimson."

"Hyssop."

"Skunk cabbage."

They threw names back and forth and pelted each other with small clumps of dirt. The battle went on until they were both rolling on the ground, dirt-smeared and laughing. He drew her face to his and kissed her through the laughter as they loved each other in the fresh soil of their garden.

And they heard the God-in-them say, "*Beloved.*"

"Oh Adam, I love you so much," Eve said. Thank you for telling me the beautiful story. Tell it again."

He told it again, then said, "The beautiful story must be planted in our garden. It will be a tree—not a fruit tree—just a plain, old, big, green tree with leafy branches, deep roots, and layers and layers of bark—an ancient tree."

"And the story of the rib, too, because I like that story a little, after all. We'll make that story a rose."

Adam grinned and nodded. "We'll have a beautiful garden

again, a garden made on earth, in earth. If we work on it and keep adding new plants, we will have enough, just enough," he said. "Roses are beautiful and also complex, with many, many layers of petals to enfold all our weeds and all our forgiveness. Roses are sacred hearts."

○

Adam and Eve did not live happily ever after. But they did live together in love, for better or worse.

And YHWH, God never had a moment's rest.

Considerations for Prayer and Reflection

"When two people love each other,
there is a third force between them. . . .
They have awakened a more ancient force around them
that will hold them together and mind them."

John O'Donohue, ANAM CARA: A BOOK OF CELTIC WISDOM

For personal prayer:

Following the guidelines for prayer described on page 16, reflect first on what the God Between might be doing between you and this midrash text:

- What got your attention?
- What brought a reaction, either positive or negative?
- Where did you feel the *hum* of the story in you?
- What relationship is the God-in-you calling you to explore through the story's characters or events?

For reflection:

People spend more time, energy—even money—on their gardens than they do on their marriages. For a good marriage or committed relationship to grow and flourish, a lot of hard work is needed, even more than it takes to cultivate a beautiful garden and keep it going. It also requires trust in the God Between, a third force to help change the lens through which two people see each other.

When a couple like Adam and Eve comes to me seeking pastoral counseling, they usually come into the room with an invisible finger pointing at each other. Younger people, especially, think their marriages were made in heaven and are as surprised as Adam and Eve when they discover that paradise is an illusion. I have often wondered, in fact, how Adam and Eve's relationship could have survived the Eden debacle. How, for that matter, does any marriage survive tragedy, chronic fear, blame, and shame?

Paradise will not be restored, nor will the honeymoon, but we shouldn't give up on the God Between. When I counsel a couple, I pray a lot and trust the reconciling power of the *third* force. And I believe that sometimes a very deep wound has within it the seeds of healing. The wound that each thinks the other has caused is often soul-shattering, but if each is willing to dare to change just a bit and put down favorite weapons, then healing can begin.

Marriage rites have questions with subtexts. Essentially, each person asks, "Will you love me, live with me, care for me for better or worse? And will you forgive the pain I know my shortcomings will inevitably inflict on our relationship?" And the other responds, "I will, with God's help." Sometimes, though, "with God's help" is omitted from the promises. We should keep it. We need it.

A good relationship, as Adam and Eve discover in this story, is like a garden, the plants of which are the mind, body, and soul of each participant. Leaving parts of the self out, including the weeds, makes the garden incomplete. By praying, by connecting with the God Between, it is easier to dare to plant all the parts of ourselves in the garden of relationship.

For further consideration on your own or in a group:

- Where do you see the healing of the God Between in Adam and Eve's marriage?

- What metaphor or image for your own relationship comes to mind? What healing does it need?

- What are the weeds in your relationship garden? What part of yourself do you leave out of your relationship?

- Has your marriage or committed relationship survived a deep wound? How?

- Is there an area where forgiveness is needed?

- How do you, or do you, pray for your marriage or committed relationship?

Idle Tale

THE WOMEN AT JESUS' TOMB

Luke 24

O

How is it that when women get together
and support each other, their collective wisdom
can make such a difference?

O

Arriving at the tomb early, the women stopped and huddled together against the cool night air to watch the dawn arrive.

"Sh-h-h-h," Faithful said.

"Who can hear us?" said Practical.

"I don't know. Just sh-h-h-h."

When the sun's light licked the horizon, Passion cried out, "Oh my God, look! Who will roll away the stone? It's huge."

The women stared at the immense obstacle and then moved closer, one by one touching the boulder that barred the entrance to the tomb where Jesus was buried.

"Oh, God, we need help," said Faithful, kneeling in front of the great stone.

"What we need is some good strong men," said Practical.

Playful laughed. "Where are they when we need them!"

Wise spoke slowly as she examined the stone, checking

it for flaws. "There might be weak spots or cracks. Can we find a way to move it?"

Bold kicked the stone. "Who chose such an enormous boulder? Didn't they figure we women would come at dawn to do our work? Didn't they think Jesus was worthy of proper burial treatment?"

"I wonder who put it here?" mused Joyful. "Probably some Roman soldiers. Our people would have known better."

The women fell silent as they contemplated the challenge before them. They had come all the way from Galilee with Jesus. They had watched him die. They had followed and seen the tomb where his body had been laid. And with no more than the exchange of a glance here and there between them, they had known they would return with spices and oils for the appropriate burial treatment.

Now, standing outside the tomb, the women looked at each other and nodded. They agreed without exchanging any words what they would do.

"Come on," said Bold.

"This is an act of love," said Passion, "so it will work. We can do it."

"And faith," said Faithful.

"And lots of divine help in our muscles," Practical said.

"And brains, too. We will move this blasted boulder. Come, help me search for branches, big branches," Bold said. "We are seven, we can do it."

"Seven all together," said Joyful.

Passion began to pray loudly as they tackled their task. "We'll roll that old stone away, yes Lord, we'll roll it on away."

"Wait," said Practical. "What if it rolls back on us and traps us?"

"Oh God," Passion leapt backward.

"Oh, girl, we'll make sure it's far enough off," said Bold.

"Women of faith," Wise said, "let's not overreact. Let's work. We can wedge these branches between the stone and the tomb's edge. But, first, we dig a hole for the stone to lean into when we push it forward. See? You four dig, and we three will get some branches. Then we all will push."

They dug and shoved and grunted and sweat. The huge boulder was finally dislodged "Okay. Rock it. Rock it. Everyone on this side. Come on. Move," shouted Bold. "Yes, there she goes." The women edged the stone into the hole they had dug.

Dawn had become day before the boulder finally slid forward and stayed in the hole. Then, with a few more shoves it rolled on down the incline and stopped several feet away from the tomb's entrance. Joyful and Playful danced around the rock and chanted, "Big bad old rock, big bad old rock. You can't keep us women out."

They all laughed, caught their breath, and rested a bit before Bold roused them and led them into the tomb's darkness.

"Do you see anything, Bold? Light the lantern, Joyful," said Wise.

"What if he's not here? Remember what he said about rising on the third day," said Practical.

"In spirit, in spirit, I think he meant," said Faithful.

"Of course, but I need to see . . . something. The spot at least," Passion moaned, clinging to Bold.

Discerning a faint shadow form, Bold shouted, "He is here. Is he here? Yes, it must be Jesus. We can begin our task, what we came for."

The other women strained to see, not quite believing.

They picked up their jars of water, oils, spices, and strips of cloth and started into the gloomy depths of the tomb, step by cautious step. For some reason, this didn't seem like the usual anointing of the dead.

As they advanced, the shadows dancing on the cave's walls became so numerous they lost sight of the form they had seen.

"Where is it?" said Practical. "I can't see it any more."

"It's right over here, I think," said Passion. "No, here." She darted around the cave. "Joyful, hold the lantern up higher." Passion moved farther into the cave, her hands beating at the air, then patting the dirt in front of her as she went. She tripped and fell forward, letting out a yell as she did.

"Passion, be careful," said Wise. "Why do you always have to do something dramatic? Get back here with us. Who knows what else lurks in this dank, dark abyss."

"Look," Joyful said, holding up the lantern. "The cave narrows. Watch out."

"I have found it," Passion said. She held up the burial cloth and kissed it as if it were as fragile as gossamer.

"What? The body?" asked Bold.

"No, silly, just the burial cloth, but Jesus must be somewhere around, close by. I'm sure," said Passion.

"Passion, the tomb isn't that big," said Bold. "And besides, how could he get out of the cloth?"

After a measured silence, Wise spoke softly. "Jesus is not here."

"Where is the body?" Practical said. "It has to be here somewhere. It has to be!"

"We'll conduct a thorough search, we'll comb every inch of this tomb," said Bold.

"Shouldn't be too hard, sister," observed Joyful, handing the lantern to Wise.

Faithful and Joyful began to feel along the walls. Practical checked the crevices at the edges. "He could have rolled down against the edge of the wall, maybe," she said.

Bold got on her hands and knees and then to her belly to crawl back into the narrow end of the cave. "Someone hold onto my feet in case the earth crumbles or there's a pit back here," Bold called to them.

"I have you, Bold," said Faithful, grabbing onto her ankles. "Go on. They could have placed him very far in."

Wise stood still in the middle of the tomb, holding the lantern. "Jesus is not here," she declared. "Not here."

Passion sat in the spot where she had fallen, holding the burial cloth and weeping.

Muddied and breathless, the group finally reassembled where Wise and Passion had remained. They sat down near each other, some of them holding onto each other's hands. Passion continued to cry, a lonely sound in the thick silence that settled itself around the little band.

After some time, Faithful whispered again, "Remember what he said."

"Shut up, Faithful, with your faithfulness," said Practical.

"But where could his body *be*? How could it get out?" said Joyful.

"Idiots! Idiots we are, groping about this dirty old rock in the ground for what? For nothing!" said Bold. "Did we lose our intelligence? We're foolishly looking for answers we obviously, obviously . . ."

" . . . could not possibly find." Wise finished her thought.

Practical put her hands to her face and sobbed. "How will we do our anointing work, our final ritual?"

"It was pretty obvious from the beginning, but we kept on looking anyway," Faithful said, putting her arm on Practical's shoulder.

"We've done all this work and come all this way for nothing. We can't even do a proper burial," said Playful with tears in her eyes.

"This is no time to belittle ourselves," Wise said firmly. "Oh God, help us to see when there is nothing to see. Save us from despair and loss of faith. We are faithful. What are we to do now? Where is Jesus? Oh God, where is he?"

They all nodded or voiced their "amens" and sat wrapped in the silence of their prayers for a long time.

Finally, Passion whispered, "It's not like we have nothing, not like there was nothing at all in here."

The others looked toward Passion who slowly unwrapped the burial cloth. She held it up for them to see, smoothing its folds across her chest. "We have this. We have this. See? It's quite amazing, beautiful, almost feels like silk. Smooth. Soft." She took an edge and stroked Wise's cheek with it. Wise managed a small smile.

"Passion, you are so eccentric!" Bold laughed. "Give me that thing." She grabbed one end of the cloth, clutching it in her fist. "What good is this old thing? What good?" Bold tried to choke back the sobs that mingled with her laugh and came from deep within her soul. Her whole body shook with the effort to contain her pain as she thumped her chest with the fist that held the edge of cloth.

"Old Bold, you're not so tough. We know," said Passion coming over to Bold. She wrapped the cloth around Bold's shoulders, held her and patted her like a baby, repeating softly, "There, there. There, there."

The rest of the company of women gathered around Bold and Passion. They held onto each other and fingered the burial cloth until they all breathed with ease and felt more peaceful.

"Well, one thing for sure is Jesus is dead . . . and we don't know where his body is. We don't know how it got out of here," Wise said.

"And we don't know what to do now, do we?" said Joyful. "And all we have is this, this . . . shroud."

"Should we take it home with us?" asked Faithful, holding the cloth close to her and kissing it.

"No, we better leave it here. As proof he was ever here to begin with," said Playful. "But I'm not ready to leave here yet, are you? I can't leave now. Let's just sit for a while and be here with the last little remembrance of Jesus we have. Okay? Maybe we'll even hear a word from Jesus. I mean, God has got to be part of this, right?"

They nodded and sat down in silence, surrounding the shroud. Each woman touched the shroud in her own way: some tentatively stroked it; some held it to their faces; others played its folds between their fingers.

"It's connecting us now, just like Jesus did when he was alive," said Passion. "Just think. This cloth wrapped the one we loved and followed, the one who gave us each new life and hope along the way."

As the women sat with the burial cloth, they harvested their memories and wove them into the soft linen fabric.

"Where is he now, do you think?" asked Practical.

"He is here," said Wise, "because we remember him and his life. It's the only way his message will stay alive. Even

though we can't do our work of anointing in the exact way we
expected, we can anoint the cloth that wrapped his body with
our remembrances. See? A little oil will make this old garment a
blessing. It's already soiled with blood and dirt. What's a little
more . . . tears, oils, spices, our own sweat." Wise grabbed a vial
of anointing oil and began to rub the edge of the burial cloth
with it.

"Make sure you rub the oils in well," Practical advised.
"It's always been women's work to tend bodies—infant bodies,
aging bodies, wounded bodies, dead bodies."

"And resurrection bodies . . ." Bold said so softly no one
heard her.

"What do you remember most about Jesus?" asked Playful. "I remember the time Jesus told Peter to get out of his
sight. Oh boy, was Peter stricken. He was so hurt. He thought
he was only protecting Jesus from thoughts of doom and death,
but Jesus was mad. He told us again that he would die."

"But none of us really believed he would die in Jerusalem, did we?" said Practical. "And you, Playful, do you remember what you did then?"

Playful giggled. "Yes. I saluted. I saluted Jesus and said,
'Yes, sir.' And he laughed. The way he laughed, I thought the
mountains would start to skip and turn somersaults. Oh, he
could be playful sometimes. And Peter relaxed, too. Didn't Jesus have a belly laugh? Oh God, I loved that guy. Do I ever miss
him! He just made life worth living."

They continued their reminiscing, laughing and crying
as they smeared oils and spices over the shroud.

"Oh, this is such a waste!" Joyful exclaimed. "I can't believe we're anointing a piece of cloth! But I remember Jesus saying it was beautiful when that woman in Bethany came in and

anointed him for burial while he was still alive. It made me cry the way he defended her and shut the others up. They were saying she was sinfully wasting the costly ointment that should be used for the poor. But Jesus said she would be remembered for all time for what she did. Do you think we'll be remembered for smearing up this old shroud?"

"Maybe we can keep it for our own memorial icon. It could be our secret," Wise said. "You know, when I think about Jesus, I picture him with all of our best qualities. He was wise—as I try to be—playful, faithful, joyful, incredibly bold, passionate, and decidedly practical. Oh, sorry. I'm rambling."

"But that's you, Wise," said Passion. "We loved to listen to Jesus talk and talk and talk, and he went on like you do. You do have wisdom. Keep on."

Wise continued as she sprinkled spices over her portion of the cloth and held it to her nose. "I remember the day he told me how impatient he often felt with even his dearest followers, how slow they seemed at times, unable to decode parables or to find grace in the midst of ordinary life. He actually told me he lost his temper far more than he wanted to, especially at poor old Peter. He told me this with tears in his eyes, almost like a confession. I told him God forgave it all, just like he told us. And you know what he said?"

"What? What?" Faithful leaned toward Wise.

"He said, 'Do *you* forgive me?' Imagine. At that moment I felt just as important as God. I felt . . ."

"Perhaps the point, hmmm?" Practical smiled. "Perhaps the point."

"You felt power," said Bold.

"It's the power of love," said Joyful. "So what did you do then?"

"She forgave him of course, darling," said Passion.

"Not exactly," Wise said.

"What! You didn't forgive Jesus?" Faithful's eyes rounded in amazement.

"I said 'not exactly.' I tried to argue about how God had forgiven him and why did he need me to, and on and on. You all know how I can go on in unwise as well as wise ways. I was so unnerved by Jesus' words that I tried to sidetrack him into a theological debate."

"But, Wise, what did Jesus say?" Faithful insisted.

"Well, three guesses, faithful Faithful," said Bold. Bold was quiet for a time and then she continued carefully. "Jesus, the one we knew and loved, would not have argued with you, Wise, but he would have listened. And he would have known that underneath you were really afraid. And then he would have done his 'fear not' thing. And then you would have not felt so afraid."

"You have it almost exactly, Bold," Wise said. "Jesus did not argue. He did listen as I burbled on. But then he said nothing. If he had said 'fear not,' I would have felt exposed, like I'd made a mistake. And you know how hard it is for me to make mistakes. So did Jesus. So he just listened and waited until I wound down my silly arguments. Looking at Jesus just standing there, not arguing with me, not leaving me, just waiting . . . that was enough, I guess, for my fear disappeared, completely gone. I don't know how it happened. For me, that was just as much of a miracle as our not finding a body in this tomb."

"For me, the miracle was when he boldly told me not to be afraid as he gripped my hand and held on tight," said Bold.

"He knew us each to the core," said Wise.

The women waited. They could see that Wise was still

reliving her own experience as she spoke. "Then I said to him, 'I forgive you, Jesus. I forgive you your weaknesses.' And then I gave him a hug, and we wept together."

"Oh, what a dear, dear memory," exclaimed Passion. "You know, as I bunch up this cloth and then smooth it out, as if I were kneading it, I can actually feel Jesus with us now. Can you? We all have our special memories of him. I've never told you mine. I'm a little embarrassed, but I remember how lovingly Jesus rejected me."

"He rejected you?" Joyful's head spun round to face Passion.

"He never rejected anyone." Faithful scowled.

"Well, he rejected me. I'll tell you about it, but you have to be quiet and listen. It's hard to tell. Some of you know the story of my younger days. You might say I had sex without thinking much about it. It was just so much fun, such a delicious pleasure." Passion looked warily around at the women. "I never thought there was anything really wrong with it, but I never could settle into one special relationship. When I met Jesus, I thought he might teach me how to get love, or how to get love and sex to go together."

"Did he?" Joyful asked.

"You didn't!" said Practical.

"Yes, I did."

"Oh my God." Playful looked shocked as she put her hand to her lips to stifle a laugh.

"I made a play for Jesus. Yes, I did. I wanted so badly to sleep with him that I forgot all about my real reasons for being a follower. Or maybe the sex was my real reason. I must say I nearly succeeded, or at least I thought I did."

"Details," Bold demanded. "Tell all."

"Jesus rejected me," Passion continued. "But I can't give details. I don't even know quite how it happened. I mean, how does someone reject someone with love? But, honest to God, that's what he did. He held me away from his body and looked at me. Seriously, into me. His eyes told me the whole thing."

"What whole thing?" Joyful asked.

"Love, silly. Love."

"Jesus said he loved you. He was in love with you?" Practical gasped.

"Not exactly," Passion answered.

"You sound like Wise now. Not exactly, but what? Get on with it," said Bold.

"Give her the time she needs," said Wise.

"Thanks," said Passion and began to wrap the cloth around her arms and face, smelling its redolence as she went. "I need to do this to help me say it. Jesus didn't tell me with his eyes or anything else that he was in love with me, and he didn't tell me precisely that he wouldn't have sex with me. He just communicated to me, maybe in the touch of his hands holding my shoulders, some, some . . . love is the only word. I can only tell you what it was like for me. I suddenly felt flooded inside and out with love, total acceptance. I knew I was perfectly beloved. Honest to God, it was better than the best of all the love I've ever had." Passion's gaze swept around the dimly lit space, taking in the faces of her sisters.

"And you know what else?" Passion said. "Jesus knew that God's own spirit had filled me with love, but he sealed it with a kiss of his own."

"No," Faithful sat straight up and stared at Passion.

"Yes, Yes. Right here." She pursed her lips to each one of her friends, and then she bent over and placed her lips on the shroud. "Pretend this is where his mouth was," she said, looking around at all of them. Then she kissed with passion.

"I am feeling what Passion said earlier," Joyful exclaimed. "I feel life in this cloth. Can you feel it, sisters? In your fingers. That's where it starts. Can you feel it now?"

Some nodded, and Faithful said as she lowered her head. "Well, he did say . . ."

"It is as if the shroud is breathing with our touch. Can you feel it?" Passion' s voice got louder.

They all nodded vigorously, but Practical said, "I'm trying, but I can't . . ."

Faithful placed her hands over Practical's hands, drew in more of the fabric to cover Practical's hands and arms and then spread it across her chest, holding it until Practical nodded. "Yes, yes. Oh, this will be *my* memory. I feel it, too. I didn't have special experiences with Jesus like the rest of you have had. I just . . . but now, just now in this dumb cloth, of all things, I feel the truth of life and love. I feel it. It's irrational, illogical, irreverent . . . not practical at all. But I feel it, the truth. Jesus is not dead. He is alive. Alive." Practical sobbed for joy.

The women stopped talking and wiped tears from their faces as they moved their hands over the cloth to feel the life. Some kissed. Some sighed. Some smiled. Some continued to weep.

"He always said God brought life out of death," Faithful spoke, breaking the silence.

"Yes," said Bold, "but we have a problem."

They all turned to look at Bold.

"Will the others believe us? I mean this 'Jesus is alive' thing? Frankly, this story from a bunch of women isn't very marketable!"

They sat in silence, all pondering the question: Who would believe the truth they knew in the intimacy of bits and pieces of shared conversation, in simple memories, in the touch of oils on cloth? This was a truth born of their senses and their intuitions. This was a mysterious, unprovable truth they knew in their flesh. Who would believe it?

"You are suggesting, I assume, that even the absence of a body isn't enough to make them believe our experience," observed Wise. "You're right, Bold. We can't assume or dismiss this question. You might even say Jesus' new life depends on it. What if they don't believe the truth we know? What if they need more proof? We know Jesus lives, but . . ."

"But how could anyone *not* believe?" said Faithful, standing up and pacing around the outside of their circle.

"As if a missing body weren't enough!" said Practical. "They might believe someone else, but they won't believe us. They'll want more proof than our word. They might not remember Jesus' words about rising from death. We, too, were slow to remember them. They won't believe!"

"The point is we have to make absolutely sure this is believed," said Joyful flatly.

"And now we won't even have a shroud because we messed it all up," sobbed Passion. "Oh God."

"We just don't have enough power, " Bold frowned.

"Are you kidding?" Wise said. "After what we've just experienced? My God, we have all the power we need. What should we do next?"

They sat silently in communion, staring lovingly at the cloth in their midst. Then Playful's silent laughter began to shake the air, a light chuckle slipping out, then erupting into full belly laughter, like the peeling of many bells.

Joyful knew this laugh and joined in. "We'll have to lie," she said, "Isn't that true?" Playful nodded. "We'll tell them the stone was removed from the entrance to the tomb when we arrived."

Faithful gasped as quiet smiles lit the women's faces.

"Not a bad little fabrication at all," commented Wise.

"Are you really suggesting we *lie*?" said Faithful. "Isn't that against the law?"

"The law says not to bear false witness. It's about testimony against your neighbor," said Wise. "But ours is a true witness. Jesus lives! It's a truth worth lying for, don't you agree? Remember what we have been given this day." She touched the cloth reverently, as if to get a last tangible piece of evidence "The truth must be preserved. We must convince the world that God's life cannot be killed or diminished. Isn't that what we felt today?" Wise looked around at the group with a sharp eye.

"Jesus died for this, you know," said Joyful. "The evil that killed him doesn't kill God's spirit. You can't keep someone like Jesus down!"

"Yes, I get it," said Passion. "The same unjust world that failed to kill Jesus' truth also will fail to keep us and ours down . . . with a little help from us."

"It's a good plan, but we all have to be on board with this," interrupted Bold.

"What do you mean, Bold? What could go wrong?" asked Passion.

"Well, we just need to make sure we tell the men that the stone was *gone* when we got here. Not that we removed it. Look at it this way. They would have real trouble believing seven weak little women removed that huge boulder, wouldn't they?" asked Bold.

They nodded.

Playful began to giggle.

"Playful gets it," said Bold smiling.

"It's easy," she sputtered through her laughing. "You see . . . they'd have more trouble believing that *we* moved the boulder than that God moved it. So God has more credibility than we do! Joke's on us."

"It's a plan, then," said Wise. "Our task is to lie for truth."

"Remember, this kind of thing isn't new," said Practical. "Think of our sisters. Rebecca lied to Isaac to make sure the right son, according to her spiritual intuition, carried the faith forward. And don't forget Judith and Esther whose manipulations saved all of us Jews."

"And Pharaoh's daughter was no slouch," said Passion, clapping her hands. "Imagine what she must have told her father when he discovered her with a Hebrew baby! Our Moses!"

"Yeah," said Bold. "Too bad the world is the way it is. God has to work around it, too. Besides, this kind of spiritual truth will have to rest secure in every breast for it to keep on bearing life. So what does it matter how we get it, or how they get it, as long as we all get it?"

"So that's our plan! Time to act." Practical called them to attention.

With a mission and a plan, they encircled Jesus' burial cloth, held hands, and began to pray in the ancient words he had told them to use:

> *Our God in heaven,*
> *holy be your name,*
> *your kingdom come,*
> *your will be done*

on earth as in heaven.
Give us today our daily bread.
Forgive us our sins
as we forgive those who sin against us.
Save us from the time of trial,
and deliver us from evil.
Amen.

One by one, the women said goodbye to the sacred cloth, which Wise carried out of the tomb with her. By now the sun was setting. A day had passed. As they went forth into the dusk, Faithful said, "This tomb is like a little temple."

"Oh my God," said Bold stopping suddenly on the path. She pointed her finger ahead of her. They all looked and saw and knew.

"The stone's still there," said Practical.

"I guess we have one more thing to do before we rest," said Wise with a heavy sigh.

"Come on," said Bold.

The women moved slowly down the incline away from the tomb's entrance to confront once more the huge stone that had blocked their entrance to Jesus. Once more they put all their minds, all their hearts, and all their bodies to the task. It was not as hard as the first time, but the seven tired women moved the great rock further along down the hill and into a group of trees where it would be unnoticed—at least by Jesus' followers who would be too excited by the good news of his life to notice it.

Having done everything well, the women left to go home. They were too exhausted for anything but hugs and smiles. Wise had left the shroud on the ground near the stone, but Faithful had seen it. Carefully, she folded it into a small bundle and tucked it neatly under the edge of the stone, thinking to herself, 'I'll tell the others later so we all will know where our shrine is.'

Tomorrow the women would tell the good news to the others. Tonight they would simply sleep in peace.

Considerations for Prayer and Reflection

"But these words seemed to them [the apostles]
an idle tale, and they did not believe them."

Luke 24:11

For personal prayer:

Following the guidelines for prayer described on page 16, reflect first on what the God Between might be doing between you and this midrash text:

- What got your attention?
- What brought a reaction, either positive or negative?
- Where did you feel the *hum* of the story in you?
- What relationship is the God-in-you calling you to explore through the story's characters or events?

For reflection:

My mother had been dead about forty minutes when I got there. She was my mother without color, flesh like gray cinders. I don't know why I kissed her dried up lips, tinged with crooked lipstick. I kissed her more than once and ran my fingers through her matted hair, over the bony ridges of her head. I hadn't touched my mother this way in life, but death freed years of longing love to pour into those kisses, into that touch, into that flesh.

Prayer is like kissing dead flesh—it is a bold act of love. It is living life on its own terms, without absolute clarity, while standing bone-naked before God. Prayerful love lets us trust our own spiritual experience. It is how I dared to kiss my dead mother. It is how I dare to stretch and plumb the scriptures in literary midrash. It is how I have let my own story, and the shared experiences of so many women, reveal ancient stories in new ways, with new perspectives.

It was with sheer delight that I listened within myself to the collective and individual experiences of the women at the tomb. These women had to be canny, I thought. They would know how important their story would be . . . and they would also know they wouldn't be the ones to write it down. I heard their voices fresh and alive, despite death and the passage of centuries. What cheered me was imagining the way they co-operated with each other, and with the God Between, to understand together their spiritual experience and to communicate in a way that could be heard and believed by others from generation to generation

I felt as if I were with the women and knew how it must have been for them there, together—with lots of faith and a big problem. I remembered being in a group of women once in which one woman shared her struggle within a very difficult relationship. The graceful thing about this particular group's way of knowing and loving was that no one offered advice or solution or judgment or, thank God, any clichés. As if there were a great, catch-all net in the middle, each woman put into the center of the gathering one or two of her own thoughts and feelings about the situation. That was all. But each of us left the group that day knowing something new and feeling strengthened by the process.

As I was writing this midrash about the women at the tomb, they lived in my psyche for a long time. They were me; they were everywoman. They needed no guidance, no spiritual direction, no pastoral counseling. To use a biblical phrase, they "disbelieved for joy" (Luke 24:41). Joy in Jesus' resurrection, and in their own. Joy in themselves, and in the spiritual power of community. I thought of big theological ideas such as resurrection, incarnation, and the communion of saints. I also thought of the work of the God Between joining death to life, woman to woman, ancient to modern. And I rejoiced.

For further consideration on your own or in a group:

- What kind of spiritual transformation do you think the God Between brought about in the group of women at the tomb?

- Have you been in a group (of women or men) in which the spirit of the God Between worked through connection and powerful things happened just because you were together?

- How does the collective wisdom of women make a difference in the life of a community? In your life?

- What is your experience of resurrection?

- Have you ever lied for truth?

About the Author

The Rev. Lyn G. Brakeman is an Episcopal priest, Pastoral Counselor and Spiritual Director with a practice in Gloucester, Massachusetts. Lyn also serves as Priest Associate at St. John's Episcopal Church in Gloucester, where her marriage partner, Dick Simeone, is the rector. She is a mentor for the Education for Ministry (EFM) program, retreat and workshop leader, a Fellow in the American Association of Pastoral Counselors, and an Associate of the Religious Sisters of Mercy. Rev. Brakeman is the author of *Spiritual Lemons: Biblical Women, Irreverent Laughter, and Righteous Rage* (Innisfree Press, 1997), which has also been published in German and Italian.

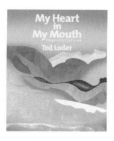